WILDLIFE
and PLANTS
of the world

An updated and expanded edition of *Wildlife of the World*

now including plants, microorganisms, and biomes

Volume 15

Taiga	902	Tomato	932
Tamarin	904	Tortoise	934
Tapir	906	Toucan	936
Tarantula	908	Tree kangaroo	938
Tasmanian devil	910	Trout	940
Tea	912	Tuna	942
Temperate forest	914	Tundra	944
Tenrec	918	Turkey	946
Termite	920	Turtle	948
Tern	922	Uakari	952
Terrapin	924	Urban habitat	954
Tide pool and coast	926	Venus flytrap	956
Tiger	928	Viper	958
Toad	930	Index	960

Marshall Cavendish
New York • London • Toronto • Sydney

Marshall Cavendish Corporation
99 White Plains Road
Tarrytown, New York 10591-9001

© Marshall Cavendish Corporation, 1999

Created by **Brown Partworks Ltd**

Library of Congress Cataloging-in-Publication Data

Wildlife and plants of the world.
    p.   cm.
    Includes bibliographical references and index.
    Summary: Alphabetically-arranged illustrated articles introduce over 350 animals, plants, and habitats and efforts to protect them.
    ISBN 0-7614-7099-9 (set : lib. bdg. : alk. paper)
    1. Animals—Juvenile literature. 2. Plants—Juvenile literature.
[1. Animals. 2. Plants.] I. Marshall Cavendish Corporation.
QL49.W539   1998
578—DC21   97-32139
                                   CIP
                                   AC

ISBN 0-7614-7099-9 (set)
ISBN 0-7614-7114-6 (vol.15)

Printed in Malaysia
Bound in the United States

Brown Packaging

Editorial consultants:
- Joshua Ginsberg, Ph.D.
- Jefferey Kaufmann, Ph.D.
- Paul Sieswerda, Ph.D.
  (Wildlife Conservation Society)
- Special thanks to the Dept. of Botany,
  The Natural History Museum, U.K.

Editors:	Deborah Evans
	Leon Gray
Assistant editor:	Amanda Harman
Art editors:	Joan Curtis
	Alison Gardner
	Sandra Horth
Picture researchers:	Amanda Baker
	Brenda Clynch
Illustrations:	Bill Botten
	John Francis

Marshall Cavendish Corporation

Editorial director:	Paul Bernabeo
Project editor:	Debra M. Jacobs
Editorial consultant:	Elizabeth Kaplan

PICTURE CREDITS

The publishers would like to thank Natural History Photographic Agency, Ardingly, Sussex, U.K., for supplying the following pictures:
Agence Nature 935, 940; A.N.T. (Bruce Thomson) 910, 911, 912, 920, 922, 938, 957; Anthony Bannister 908, 921, 954, 955; G. I. Bernard 933; Joe B. Blossom 925; James H. Carmichael Jr. 936; Stephen Dalton 905, 917, 954, 955, 937; Robert J. Erwin 930; Patrick Fagot 928; P. German 939; Daniel Heuclin 956, 931; T. Kitchin & V. Hurst 903, 945; Hellio & Van Ingen 924; E. A. Janes 904; Peter Johnson 919; Ralph & Daphne Keller 913; Stephen Krasemann 916, 934, 948, 949; Gerard Lacz 929; Lutra 941; Eero Murtomaki 902; Haroldo Palo 952; Rod Planck 915; Jany Sauvenet 906, 951, 953; Kevin Schafer 907; John Shaw 909, 914, 918, 946, 947; R. Sorensen & J. Olsen 944; Morten Strange 950; A. Williams 923; Norbert Wu 919.

Additional pictures supplied by:
Frank Lane Picture Agency 918, 942; Image Bank 932; Planet Earth Pictures 943.

Front cover
Main image: Red-billed toucan, photographed by Stephen Dalton.
Additional image: Ripening tomatoes, photographed by G. I. Bernard.

Status

In the Key Facts on the species described in this publication, you will find details of the appearance, name (both Latin and common name wherever possible), breeding habits, and so on. The status of an organism indicates how common it is. The status of each organism is based on reference works prepared by two organizations: *1996 IUCN Red List of Threatened Animals* published by the International Union for Conservation of Nature and Natural Resources (IUCN) and *Endangered and Threatened Wildlife and Plants* published in 1997 by the United States Government Printing Office (USGPO)

Extinct:	No sighting in the last 40 years
Endangered:	In danger of becoming extinct
Threatened:	A species that will become endangered if its present condition in the wild continues to deteriorate
Rare:	Not threatened, but not frequently found in the wild
In captivity:	A species that is extinct in the wild but has been kept successfully in captivity
Feral:	Animals that have been domesticated and have escaped into the wild
Common:	Frequently found within its range, which may be limited
Widespread:	Commonly found in many parts of the world

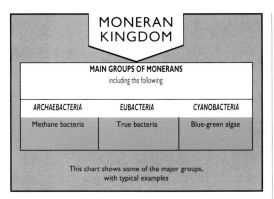

MONERAN KINGDOM

MAIN GROUPS OF MONERANS
including the following:

ARCHAEBACTERIA	EUBACTERIA	CYANOBACTERIA
Methane bacteria	True bacteria	Blue-green algae

This chart shows some of the major groups, with typical examples

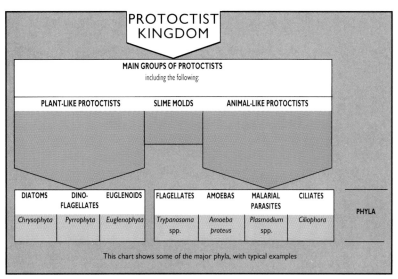

PROTOCTIST KINGDOM

MAIN GROUPS OF PROTOCTISTS
including the following:

PLANT-LIKE PROTOCTISTS			SLIME MOLDS	ANIMAL-LIKE PROTOCTISTS			
DIATOMS	DINO-FLAGELLATES	EUGLENOIDS		FLAGELLATES	AMOEBAS	MALARIAL PARASITES	CILIATES
Chrysophyta	*Pyrrophyta*	*Euglenophyta*		*Trypanosoma* spp.	*Amoeba proteus*	*Plasmodium* spp.	*Ciliophora*

PHYLA

This chart shows some of the major phyla, with typical examples

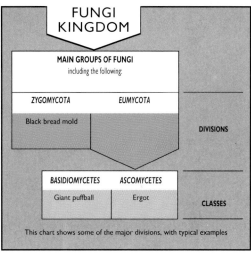

FUNGI KINGDOM

MAIN GROUPS OF FUNGI
including the following:

ZYGOMYCOTA	EUMYCOTA
Black bread mold	

DIVISIONS

BASIDIOMYCETES	ASCOMYCETES
Giant puffball	Ergot

CLASSES

This chart shows some of the major divisions, with typical examples

Moneran, protoctist, and fungi kingdoms

Three groups of living things are not classified in the animal and plant kingdoms. These are the moneran, protoctist, and fungi kingdoms. Monerans are tiny, single-celled organisms that have no distinct nucleus. The nucleus is the control center of the cell. In contrast, protoctists and fungi have visibly distinct nuclei and tiny organs (called organelles). However, classification is a topic for much debate, and many scientists disagree on the classification of organisms in these three kingdoms.

The moneran kingdom contains all the microscopic, single-celled organisms that do not have distinct nuclei. The three main groups of monerans are: true bacteria, blue-green algae, and methane bacteria. The largest group of monerans is the true bacteria (*Eubacteria*).

For over a billion years, bacteria were the only living things on the earth. Then about 1.5 billion years ago, new organisms, called protoctists (formerly known as protists), evolved from the methane bacteria. All protoctists are single-celled organisms, but their cell structure is more complex than monerans. For example, protoctists have nuclei.

Scientists tend to classify an organism as a protoctist when they cannot place the organism in the animal, plant, or fungi kingdoms. Protoctists are grouped into phyla that have animal-, plant-, or fungus-like features. Single-celled algae, such as diatoms and euglenoids, behave like plants. Amoebas can move about and are more like animals. Slime molds form a subkingdom that have characteristics similar to the fungi kingdom.

Fungi make up the last kingdom of living things. Mushrooms, toadstools, and molds are all fungi. Fungi differ from animals and plants in that they depend on other organisms for their food. Like plants, fungi form groups called divisions. There are two divisions in the fungi kingdom.

See Volume 17 for more information on monerans, protoctists, and fungi.

COLOR GUIDE

MONERANS, PROTOCTISTS, & FUNGI

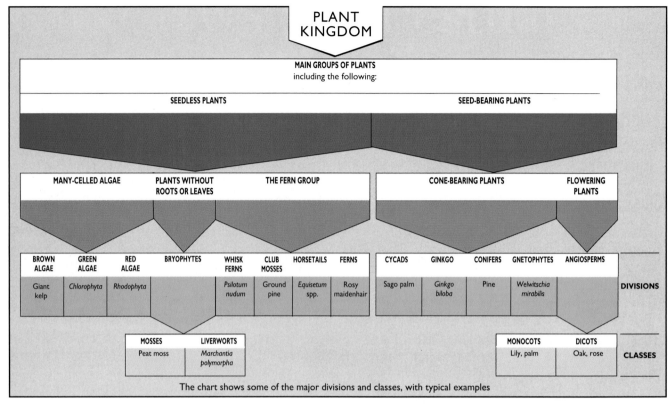

The chart shows some of the major divisions and classes, with typical examples

The plant kingdom

Every plant, from the tiniest shrub to the tallest tree, belongs to the plant kingdom. There are about 500,000 different kinds (species) of plant that have been identified.

The plant kingdom (shown above) can be divided into 13 divisions. A plant division is similar to a phylum in animal classification. Each division represents a number of classes of plants that all have certain features in common.

The simplest plants are algae, all of which live in water. This set of books classifies three divisions of multicellular (or many-celled) algae in the plant kingdom. Some scientists, though, prefer to classify multicellular algae as protoctists.

Two classes, mosses and liverworts, make up the bryophyte division. These plants lack the roots, stems, and leaves that are found in other plant divisions.

The fern group comprises four divisions of the plant kingdom: whisk ferns, club mosses, horsetails, and ferns. All members of the fern group have two stages in their life cycle. During one of these stages tiny reproductive structures, called spores, are released. These spores will eventually grow into a new plant.

More complex plants reproduce with seeds. Four divisions of plants reproduce with "naked" seeds in cones. Cycads, conifers, ginkgoes, and gnetophytes are all cone-bearing plants.

Two classes, monocots and dicots, make up the largest division of plants, the angiosperms, or flowering plants. Unlike cone-bearing plants, angiosperms reproduce with enclosed seeds such as berries, nuts, and fruits.

See Volume 17 for more information on the different divisions of plants.

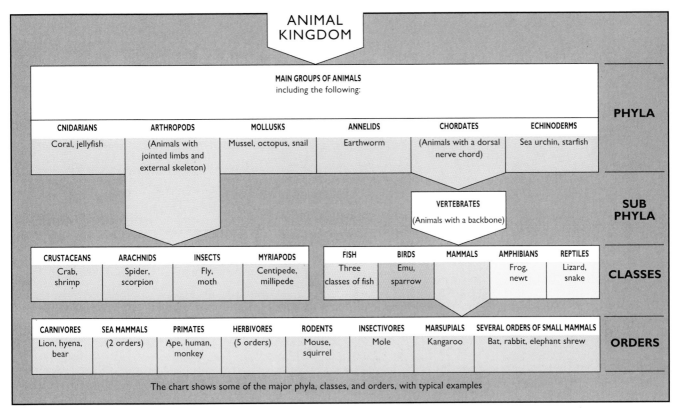

ANIMAL KINGDOM

MAIN GROUPS OF ANIMALS including the following:						PHYLA
CNIDARIANS Coral, jellyfish	**ARTHROPODS** (Animals with jointed limbs and external skeleton)	**MOLLUSKS** Mussel, octopus, snail	**ANNELIDS** Earthworm	**CHORDATES** (Animals with a dorsal nerve chord)	**ECHINODERMS** Sea urchin, starfish	

VERTEBRATES (Animals with a backbone) — SUB PHYLA

CRUSTACEANS	ARACHNIDS	INSECTS	MYRIAPODS	FISH	BIRDS	MAMMALS	AMPHIBIANS	REPTILES	CLASSES
Crab, shrimp	Spider, scorpion	Fly, moth	Centipede, millipede	Three classes of fish	Emu, sparrow		Frog, newt	Lizard, snake	

CARNIVORES	SEA MAMMALS	PRIMATES	HERBIVORES	RODENTS	INSECTIVORES	MARSUPIALS	SEVERAL ORDERS OF SMALL MAMMALS	ORDERS
Lion, hyena, bear	(2 orders)	Ape, human, monkey	(5 orders)	Mouse, squirrel	Mole	Kangaroo	Bat, rabbit, elephant shrew	

The chart shows some of the major phyla, classes, and orders, with typical examples

The animal kingdom

In the eighteenth century, a botanist from Sweden named Carl von Linné (usually known by his Latin name, *Carolus Linneaus*) outlined a system of classifying plants and animals. This became the basis for classification all over the world. Scientists use Latin names so that all plants, animals, and other living things can be identified accurately, even though they have different common names in different places. Linneaus divided living organisms into two kingdoms: plants and animals. Today most scientists divide living things into five kingdoms: animals, plants, monerans, protoctists, and fungi. The animal kingdom (*above*) is divided into many phyla. Most of the phyla of the animal kingdom contain strange creatures — microscopic organisms, sponges, corals, slugs, and insects — without the backbone and central nervous system that we associate with more familiar animals.

Each phylum is divided into classes. For example, vertebrates (animals with a backbone) are a subdivision of a phylum and are divided up into seven classes: mammals, birds, reptiles, amphibians, and three classes of fish (represented by eels, sharks, and trout).

Each of these classes is broken down further into different orders. The mammal class, for instance, includes the orders carnivores (meat eaters), insectivores (insect eaters), primates (monkeys, apes), and marsupials (kangaroos, koalas), among others.

In this set of books, we give Latin names for different groups (genera) and kinds (species) of animals. See Volume 17 for more information on the different phyla of animals.

COLOR GUIDE

INVERTEBRATES

FISH

AMPHIBIANS & REPTILES

BIRDS

MAMMALS

PLANTS

BIOMES & HABITATS

MONERANS, PROTOCTISTS, & FUNGI

Taiga

The taiga is found only in the northern hemisphere, stretching from Alaska through Canada, Scandinavia, and northwestern Russia to Siberia. It is the world's largest forest biome and is dotted with large lakes, bogs, and wooded swamps.

Taiga forests developed as ice receded from the area at the end of the last Ice Age. Its relative youth and the harsh environment mean there is little variety in species native to the taiga.

Flora

The taiga forests consist mainly of coniferous trees. These trees are well adapted to the extremes of climate, low light and temperature levels, and nutrient-poor soils that characterize the habitat. Pine needles decompose slowly when they fall to the floor, and they do not return nutrients to the soil. As a result, the ground is dominated by plants (such as ferns and mosses) and lichens, which can thrive in nutrient-poor soils.

To obtain the nutrients they need, conifers have developed a close relationship with lichens. Lichens are actually two different organisms: a fungus and an alga. The algae cells use energy from sunlight to make food in a process called photosynthesis. The trees take some of this food for themselves. In return, the trees provide shelter for the lichens.

Changing seasons

The relatively warm growing season in the taiga is less than 120 days, but the dark, cold winter season is more than six months long. High winds and snow are typical of this cold season, and the water in the soil is frozen except during the brief summer season.

Only the top layer of soil thaws in the summer, so the root systems of trees are usually shallow. In winter, growth almost stops. Larches grow in the coldest regions of the taiga. Unusually for conifers, however, larches are deciduous trees, which means they lose their needle-like leaves in the winter. The Dahurian larch (*Larix dahurica*) is widespread in Eastern

◄ *When space and light allow, broadleaved, deciduous trees will start to colonize the taiga's coniferous forests.*

KEY FACTS

- **Location**
  The northern hemisphere from Alaska and Canada across Europe and Asia to eastern Siberia

- **Temperature ranges**
  50°F (10°C) in the warmest months, dropping to less than 32°F (0°C) in winter

- **Annual precipitation**
  Varies from 10 to 20 in (25 to 50 cm)

- **Typical flora**
  Alders, aspens, birches, ferns, firs, larches, lichens, pines, and spruces

- **Typical animals**
  Adder, American mink, beaver, Brown bear, capercaillie, caribou, Common toad, ermine, goshawk, Gray wolf, grouse, lynx, moose, Northern flying squirrel, sable, vole

Siberia and experiences the most extreme temperature variations of the taiga.

Spruces and firs are found mostly in the northern part of the taiga's range, whereas pines are common in the southern areas. Conifers are better adapted to cope with strong winds and snow than deciduous trees. The branches of conifers slope down to stop snow from sticking. The branches are also relatively flexible and grow close together, which shields the trees from high winds. Their thick bark protects them from cold, fire, and insect pests.

Animals in the taiga

Large mammals, such as the moose (*Alces alces*), Brown bear (*Ursus ursus*), and Gray wolf (*Canis lupus*), make the taiga their home, as do smaller species such as the beaver (*Castor* spp.). All have thick fur to help them survive the cold. Smaller mammals, such as the Northern flying squirrel (*Glaucomys volans*), tend to hibernate, or sleep, through the winter.

In Europe and Asia, birds such as the capercaillie (*Tetrao urogallus*) feed on berries and needles from the trees. The goshawk (*Accipiter gentilis*) and other birds

of prey are common to the taiga. Smaller birds migrate south during the winter.

Few reptiles and amphibians can survive the cold environment of the taiga. However, there are some species, such as the adder (*Vipera berus*) and the Common toad (*Bufo bufo*), to be found there.

Humans in the taiga

The fur trade is a real threat to some rare taiga species. The pelts of Black bears (*Ursus americanus*) and the lynx (*Felis lynx*) are highly prized, although both animals are now protected by law. American mink (*Mustela vison*) and sable (*Martes zibellina*) are now farmed rather than hunted.

Softwoods are the main harvest, and logging is common in many taiga forests. However, most of this attractive habitat is largely untouched, because the nutrient-poor soil is not suited to farming.

▲ *These Brown, or Grizzly, bears (**Ursus ursus**) are quite at home in the taiga, with their thick coats to protect them against the cold. These bears are hunting for fish in the Katmai National Park, Alaska.*

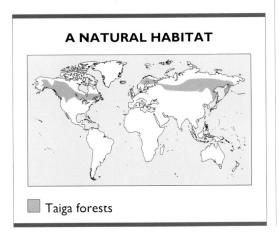

A NATURAL HABITAT

☐ Taiga forests

See also **Bear, Larch, Lichen, Lynx, Pine**

Tamarin

Tamarins are small, distinctive, squirrel-like monkeys with long tails and silky coats decorated with brightly colored tufts, manes, and mustaches. Closely related to the marmosets, there are 15 species of tamarin altogether living in tropical rainforests throughout South America. Many of these species are now rare or threatened, mainly due to destruction of much of their rainforest habitat. In particular, the lion tamarins of Brazil (*Leontopithecus* species) are endangered and may be facing extinction.

There are three species of lion tamarin: the Golden lion tamarin, the Black lion tamarin, and the Golden-headed tamarin. They were formerly thought to be subspecies of one species. Lion tamarins

are the largest of the tamarins and marmosets, growing up to 16 in (40 cm) from head to rump, with long, flowing tails of 15 in (38 cm).

Traveling through the rainforests

Diurnal animals (active during the day), tamarins spend the nighttime sleeping in treeholes, thick vegetation, or tangles of creepers in the dense rainforests. During the day they spend their time in family groups of 4-15 animals, running along the

▼ *One of the three species of Lion tamarin, the Golden lion tamarin* (Lontopithecus rosalia) *is the only species to be completely golden in color. It has a fantastic, bushy mane surrounding its small, impish face.*

KEY FACTS

- **Name**
  Golden lion tamarin
  (*Leontopithecus rosalia*)

- **Range**
  Brazil

- **Habitat**
  Tropical forests

- **Appearance**
  The largest of the tamarins, measuring up to 16 in (40 cm) from head to rump, with a tail of 15 in (38 cm); a thick and bushy golden mane surrounds the face, covering the ears; the coat is golden in color; closely related species vary slightly in color

- **Food**
  Fruit, flowers, plant gum and nectar, insects, frogs, lizards, snails, small birds

- **Breeding**
  Female gives birth to 1-2 young (usually twins), about $4\frac{1}{2}$ months after mating; the mother suckles them, but most of the parental care is undertaken by the father

- **Status**
  Endangered

branches and leaping nimbly from tree to tree high in the canopy, and calling to each other with high-pitched sounds almost like birdsong. For 25-30 percent of this time the tamarins forage for food, and much of the rest of the day is spent in grooming each other, particularly the parents and their most recent offspring.

Tamarins are very territorial, constantly scent-marking home ranges that cover 25-100 acres (10-40 ha). Each day the groups of tamarins visit about one third of their territories, traveling as far as 1.2 miles (2 km). They feed on a wide range of foods, from fruit, flowers, and nectar to animal prey such as reptiles, amphibians, spiders, and insects. Indeed, Lion tamarins have especially long hands and fingers for searching through vegetation and reaching into treeholes in order to catch small invertebrates.

NATURAL HABITAT

Golden lion tamarin

▲ *It is very easy to see why this strange creature is called the* **Cotton-top tamarin** *(Saguinus oedipus), with its bushy mop of white hair. This species also has a very distinctive call or song, and is sometimes known as the* **Nightingale monkey.**

Only one mother

As in marmosets, only one female tamarin in any family group breeds at a time, although she may mate with any of the adult males. Twice a year, about four months after mating, the breeding female gives birth to nonidentical twins. These babies are very small when they are born (around 9-15 percent of their mother's weight) and are completely dependent on their parents. For the first seven to ten days, the other members of the group help in carrying and feeding the young, after which the babies have developed enough to move around on their own. Once they become adult, they remain in the family group to help their parents raise their younger brothers and sisters.

See also **Marmoset**

Tapir

The tapir's massive, stocky body is rounded at the rump and tapers into a long, pointed face at the front, enabling it to move quickly through dense forest undergrowth. Its legs are quite short and slender, and its tail is small and stumpy. There are four species of tapir: three are found in the forests of Central and South America and one in Southeast Asia. They belong to a group of animals known as odd-toed ungulates and are most closely related to horses, zebra, and rhinoceroses.

All species of tapir have little hair covering their thick, leathery hides, except for the Mountain tapir (*Tapirus pinchaque*), which has a thick coat of coarse bristles to protect it from the cold. The Malayan tapir (*Tapirus indicus*) is black on the front half of its body and hind legs, and white everywhere else. This breaks up the animal's outline to help camouflage it in the dark forests at night and to protect it from nighttime predators. The other three

▲ *The Brazilian tapir can use its long nose to grasp leaves and other food.*

species are all uniformly brown-black. The Malayan tapir is also the largest species, measuring as much as 8 ft (2.4 m) from head to rump.

The tapir's snout is like a miniature elephant's trunk. The long upper lip forms this fleshy nose, which, like the elephant's trunk, is excellent for grasping leaves and fruit. This trunk is most developed in the Baird's tapir (*Tapirus bairdii*), a rare animal found in the swampy forests of Mexico and Central America.

Water-loving animals

All tapirs live in forest habitats, usually close to water. Despite their short legs, they are excellent swimmers and spend so much time in water that they have even been known to mate while submerged beneath the surface. Like pigs, peccaries, and hippos, tapirs also enjoy mud baths. The mud not only keeps the tapirs cool in the steamy heat of the forests, but also helps remove parasites such as ticks that carry disease and annoy the animals. After leaving the mud wallows, tapirs often rub

NATURAL HABITAT

Brazilian tapir

themselves against tree trunks to scrape off the suffocated ticks.

Like many forest animals whose food is spread widely throughout their range, tapirs live a solitary life, with only a mother and her young remaining together for any length of time. They usually feed at night, and eat most kinds of plant food, grazing on grass and browsing on leaves, buds, twigs, and fruit. They also eat vegetation growing in water – not surprising given the amount of time they spend there. They use their trunk-like noses to sniff out food and, like hands, to place it into their mouths when feeding.

Tapirs can breed at any time of the year. The gestation period (the time that the baby is growing inside its mother) in these animals is quite long – about 13 or 14 months. Before giving birth the female finds a safe, sheltered spot. She gives birth to one young, rarely two. The offspring are born with their eyes open and can walk soon after birth. For the first week or so the young are left in a sheltered spot while the mother goes out feeding, then they start to accompany her on excursions. They stay with her for 10 to 11 months before becoming independent.

Almost extinct

Tapirs were once fairly common animals, with a much wider range than they have today. In the past they were found in North America, and they lived on the Florida peninsula until about 11,000 years ago. The disappearance of tapirs over much of their range coincided with the arrival of humans in the New World. Today, many scientists believe that tapirs

(along with many other species of large mammals) became extinct because they were overhunted by these early human migrants. Tapirs were easy targets for early hunters. Despite their size – some species weigh up to 650 lb (295 kg) – tapirs are usually shy and docile, and in zoos they quickly become very tame. When frightened in the wild, they tend to run into the forest or hide in the water, making them vulnerable to attack by human hunters.

Today all four species of tapir are endangered and may be facing extinction. This is mainly due to loss of habitat through the clearing of forests for farmland, as well as from hunting. Although humans are their principal enemy, the tapir's natural predators are big cats such as mountain lions and jaguars in the Americas and tigers in Asia.

KEY FACTS

- **Name**
  Brazilian or South American tapir (*Tapirus terrestris*)

- **Range**
  South America: from Colombia and Venezuela to northern Argentina and southern Brazil

- **Habitat**
  Tropical rainforests; woodlands or grasslands close to water

- **Appearance**
  Body length 6-7 ft (1.8-2.2 m); the body color is dark grayish-brown to reddish-brown; a short, upright mane

- **Food**
  Plant material, especially fruit

- **Breeding**
  Single young (rarely 2) is born 13-14 months after mating; it stays with its mother for 10-11 months

- **Status**
  Endangered

◄ *This young tapir's brown coat and pale markings camouflage it in the speckled light of the forest floor.*

907

Tarantula

Tarantulas are large, hairy spiders that are almost universally feared, even by people who are not usually frightened of spiders. The first spider to be called a tarantula was the tarantula *Lycosa tarantula* from southern Europe. It was named after the Italian town of Taranto where it was found. In the fifteenth century it was believed that a bite from this spider would lead to madness and that the only way to get the spider's poison out of the body was to dance a frenzied dance, the tarantella. However, tarantula is now the common name given to many members of the *Mygalomorph* group of spiders that is found in North, Central, and South America, Australia, and other hot places.

Fearsome sights

Tarantulas are nocturnal creatures, hiding away in crevices and burrows during the day and only coming out to hunt at night. They live in a variety of habitats, from deep burrows in the ground to silken

KEY FACTS

- **Name**
  Desert tarantula
  (*Aphonopelma chalcodes*)

- **Range**
  Arizona, New Mexico, and southern California

- **Habitat**
  Desert

- **Appearance**
  2-2$\frac{3}{4}$ in (5-7 cm) long; a brown body and legs covered with golden hairs

- **Food**
  Insects, lizards, and other small vertebrates

- **Breeding**
  Male searches for a female; after mating the female lays eggs in an egg capsule and leaves it hidden in a natural cavity; spiderlings look like miniature adults

- **Status**
  Rare

◄ *This tarantula has seized a grasshopper outside its burrow. The entrance is like a tunnel of silk.*

tubes high up in the trees. They are usually brown or black, and they have hairs on their bodies and legs that pick up information about their surroundings. These hairs can sense movements and chemicals that might indicate other creatures are about. The largest tarantula, the Goliath bird-eating spider *(Theraphosa leblondi)* from the swamps of Guyana, Surinam, and Venezuela, may have a leg span of 10 in (25 cm).

Most species lie in wait for their prey to come along and then suddenly jump on it. Others may wander in search of prey. The bird-eating spiders of Colombia, Peru, and Bolivia, for example, creep around the branches of the rainforest in search of female birds sitting on their nests, tending their eggs. Other tarantulas eat a variety of prey, including snakes and lizards.

Most tarantulas poison their prey with fangs. Not all tarantulas are poisonous to humans, but some, including the Goliath bird-eating spider, have hairs that are very irritating to mammals (including humans). In fact, this spider can rub the hairs off its legs if it feels threatened, and the hairs float off in the breeze to travel up the nose of a predator. This form of defense warns the predator not to approach the next large, hairy spider it meets.

Down south

In the U.S., one of the best known tarantulas is the Desert tarantula. This light brown spider is well disguised against its sandy surroundings. Like other tarantulas (and most spiders) the female is larger than the male. The male has to search for a female that is ready to mate.

He must be wary, and in many cases the male becomes a meal rather than a mate. He pins the female down and passes a sac of sperm to her. The female then lays an egg sac in her burrow. The spiderlings hatch after about two months and there may be as many as 700 in each egg sac. Male tarantulas are not long lived, but females can survive for 25 years.

Several species are becoming rare due to habitat loss and overcollecting for the pet trade. The best known pet spider is the Mexican red knee *(Brachypelma smithi)*.

▲ *Like other species, this Desert tarantuala in Arizona has special hairs on its legs that sense chemicals in the air.*

NATURAL HABITAT

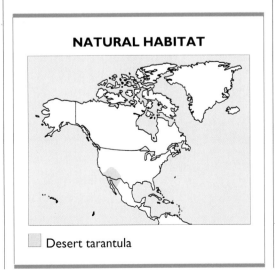

Desert tarantula

See also **Spider**

Tasmanian devil

The Tasmanian devil is a small bear- or dog-like marsupial that is found only on the island of Tasmania, off the mainland of Australia. It is a carnivore (meat eater) and, with its large, sharp teeth and powerful jaws, has a reputation for being extremely ferocious. This reputation, along with its dark, black coat and the pinkness of its snout and ears, caused some people to think of a devil when they saw it – hence its common name.

Tasmanian devils are nocturnal animals (active at night), and they spend the day resting in special nests in caves, hollow logs, thick vegetation, or holes deserted by other animals such as wombats. These nests are made by both females and males, using bark, grass, and leaves. At night the Tasmanian devils come out of their resting places to hunt for food. They are solitary hunters, with males and females getting together only during the breeding season.

With their small, rounded bodies, Tasmanian devils usually move fairly slowly and clumsily, although they can run at up to 8 mph (13 km/h) when necessary. This may be when chasing prey such as kangaroo rats, birds, snakes, and frogs. However, they are not very efficient hunters compared to many other carnivores, needing to give several savage bites to a victim's back or neck before killing it, and they prefer to eat carrion (the meat of dead animals) when possible.

An exaggerated reputation

Indeed, the Tasmanian devils' reputation for viciousness is largely exaggerated, extending mainly to squabbles between themselves over carcasses. Even then they simply growl and screech and do not usually attack each other. However, they are voracious eaters, and their large, sharp

▲ *This female Tasmanian devil is jealously guarding her two offspring. As soon as they are old enough, they will be able to leave the nest and ride on their mother's back as she forages for food.*

▶ *This ferocious Tasmanian devil shows off its sharp teeth. It has a reputation in some areas for killing sheep, but in fact it usually eats only dead sheep or occasionally kills and eats sick lambs.*

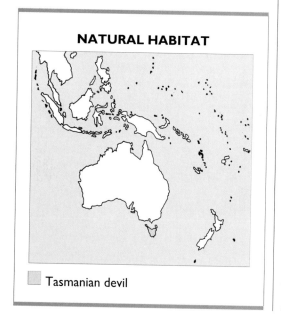

NATURAL HABITAT

☐ Tasmanian devil

teeth and powerful jaws allow them to chew through every part of a carcass, including the bones! They usually feed on dead sheep, kangaroos, rabbits, wombats, and wallabies.

Living in a pouch

Mating among Tasmanian devils usually occurs once a year from March to April, and the female gives birth to one litter of two to four young about a month later. As is the case in other marsupials, the offspring are very poorly developed at birth and continue to grow in a special pouch on their mother's abdomen, where they suckle from her teats.

Once they reach the age of about 15 weeks, the young start to leave the pouch and stay in the nest while their mother goes foraging for food. As they get older, they may accompany her on these foraging trips, riding on her back. They are weaned at eight months old and become fully adult at about two years. Tasmanian devils usually live to a maximum age of seven or eight years.

Tasmanian devils once occupied much of Australia as well as Tasmania, only dying out with the introduction of the dingo thousands of years ago, with which it had to compete for food. In Tasmania, where there are no dingoes, the Tasmanian devil seems to have benefited from European settlement as a result of the increased number of carcasses available – from dead farm animals and roadkills, for example.

KEY FACTS

- **Name**
  Tasmanian devil
  (*Sarcophilus harrisii*)

- **Range**
  Tasmania

- **Habitat**
  Most habitats except very open ground

- **Appearance**
  A small marsupial, measuring 20-25 in (55-65 cm) from head to rump, with a tail of 9½-10 in (24.5-26 cm); black or blackish-brown fur with a white throat; a big head with powerful jaws and large, strong teeth; large, pink ears and a pinkish snout

- **Food**
  Small mammals, reptiles, fish, invertebrates; often eats carrion (dead meat)

- **Breeding**
  Mating occurs from March-April; one month later the female gives birth to a litter of 2-4 young; these are poorly developed at birth and continue to grow inside their mother's pouch; they are weaned at 8 months

- **Status**
  Common

Tea

Legend tells us that tea was first brewed from the leaves of a *Camellia* plant in China about 5000 years ago. Originally, it was used for medicine. However, tea was so tasty that by the 3rd century A.D. the Chinese drank it for pleasure every day.

In 1610, the Dutch East India Company brought the first shipment of China tea to Europe. Fifty years later, the British East India Company imported tea to London. The first teas to reach England were China teas, but the British quickly discovered, and cultivated, the superb Assam tea that grows in northern India.

Classification of teas

Different teas have different flavors and aromas. Most modern teas are blends of several kinds of tea leaves. Blending tea is an art, and the right kinds of tea must be used. Teas are classified by their origin. There is China tea, Ceylon tea, Japanese tea, and African tea. India's teas are classified by their native state: Assam or Darjeeling. Teas are also classified by whether or not they are fermented, or processed with chemicals. China's green tea is not fermented. Our popular black, Assam tea, is a fermented tea.

The size of the leaves used to make a tea blend is also important. Large-leaf grades of tea are made with the tougher, more mature leaves of the plant. Broken-leaf grades of tea are made with young, tender shoots. Today nearly all tea comes from broken grades, which produce a strong brew quickly.

The tea plant

There are about 80 species of evergreen shrubs and trees in the *Theaceae* or tea plant family. Tea plants are in the group (genus) *Camellia*. Assam tea, *Camellia sinensis* var. *assamica*, comes from a tree that has shiny, green, oval leaves that are roughly 1-8 in (3-20 cm) long. Naturally, tea trees would grow to be 50 ft (15 m) tall. On plantations, however, the trees are trimmed to keep them shrubby. Like all *Camellia* species, tea trees produce rose-like, showy flowers. Fragrant Assam tea tree flowers are about 1½ in (4 cm) wide and have between five and seven white petals.

▲ *On tea plantations trees are trimmed to keep them at a convenient height for picking and to encourage the growth of tender, new leaves.*

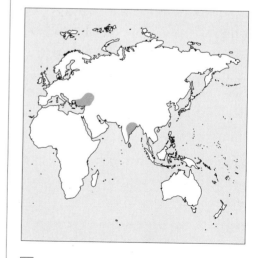

NATURAL HABITAT

■ Original range of Assam tea

Processing tea

Tea processing has two goals: to dry the leaf and to bring out its best qualities, based on the chemicals in the leaf. One chemical is caffeine (a stimulant also in coffee). Other important ingredients in tea leaves are substances known as polyphenols in the sap, which help give tea its strong flavor. The leaves of different tea plants also contain oils that give each one a unique flavor and aroma.

Withering and rolling

Tea leaves begin to wither when they are plucked from the tree. They lose water and become limp. Workers aid the withering process by laying picked leaves out on special trays for open-air drying. More often, the tea leaves are withered, or dried, in machines. Leaves are spread out on mesh or moving belts, or are put in punctured drums and then blasted with hot air. Machine withering saves time and money but can help to destroy some of the leaf chemicals that give tea its fine flavor and scent.

If you have ever seen loose tea in tins, you may have wondered why the leaves are so tightly curled up. Tea leaves get twisted during the rolling process. When they are rolled (by hand or with machines), the leaf cells burst open. This allows the chemicals in the leaf to mix together and react with each other.

Fermentation and drying

After the rolling process, the tea leaves are sieved and spread out on trays for fermentation. Temperature, humidity, and air movement are carefully controlled.

The tea leaves turn a characteristic red or red-brown color, and their aroma develops. Heat is then applied to the fermented tea leaves to dry them out. Most drying is done in machines through which hot air is passed.

Packaging tea

Processed tea is graded by the color, size, and shape of the leaf particles. Grading is done by machines that sift the processed leaves. The final product is packed in bulk in large, lined wooden chests. Chests are sealed to prevent moisture from damaging the leaves. Bulk tea may be shipped to packagers. There, tea tasters may sample various leaf brews to insure high quality. Then different teas may be blended. Some tea is packaged in small tins and sold loose.

Tea bags are made out of a special porous paper that allows air and water to flow through it. Machines are used to pack and seal highly broken-leaf tea blends in bags. Quality teas are blends of as many as 40 different kinds of tea.

KEY FACTS

● **Name**
Assam tea (*Camellia sinensis* var. *assamica*)

● **Range**
Assam (northeastern India), Burma, Sri Lanka, Thailand, China, Vietnam

● **Habitat**
Grown in plantations in subtropical highlands and mountainous regions

● **Appearance**
Wild, evergreen tree to 50 ft (15 m); glossy green oval leaves 1-8 in (3-20 cm) long; showy, white flowers with 5-7 petals, 1½ in (4 cm) wide

● **Life cycle**
Perennial

● **Uses**
Leaves blended and brewed with water to make tea

● **Status**
Common in cultivation

◄ *Young leaves of tea are carefully picked by hand so that the leaves are not bruised or damaged.*

See also **Coffee**

Temperate forest

As the name implies, temperate forests are found in the temperate zone. These forests occur mainly across North America, Europe, and Asia. However, some areas of South America, Africa, and Australia are covered by temperate forests. Generally a temperate forest requires a minimum of four frost-free months and, on average, the rainfall is 75 to 250 cm (30 to 100 in), falling regularly throughout the year. In winter, the rain usually falls as snow.

Once there were great swathes of deciduous and evergreen forests covering the continents within the temperate zone, but most of these have been cut back by humans to make way for cities, towns,

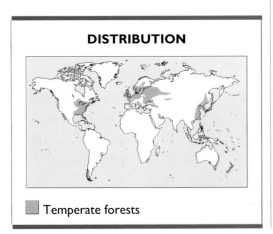

DISTRIBUTION

Temperate forests

▲ *The Blue Ridge Parkway in the Smoky Mountains National Park, North Carolina, is typical of deciduous, temperate forests. Rhododendrons have broken through a gap in the canopy in search of light, and some evergreen trees have also colonized the forest.*

villages, and agricultural land. Now there are only a few isolated patches of woodland left within the temperate forest habitat. In eastern North America, temperate forests stretch roughly from the eastern seaboard across to the Mississippi River, and from the Gulf of Mexico up to the Great Lakes. In the west, the forests extend from Alaska to roughly halfway down the California coast.

Types of temperate forest

There are four different types of temperate forest: deciduous, evergreen, mixed, and temperate rainforest. Most forests in the temperate zone are called deciduous forests because their trees shed their leaves during the fall in preparation for the winter. This allows the trees to save energy by becoming dormant until the spring, when new leaves sprout, and the trees can begin to flourish again. The main type of tree varies from place to place. For example, the eastern slopes of the Appalachian Mountains are covered in oak forests, while in the upper Midwest the forests are made up mainly of American basswoods and Sugar maples. In the southeastern states the most common forest trees are oaks and hickories.

In contrast, trees in the temperate evergreen forest keep their leaves all through the changing seasons. Evergreen trees such as pine, fir, and hemlock are found in the forests of the Rocky Mountains and in the Sierra Nevadas. These coniferous trees have needle-like leaves. The evergreen forests of Australia, New Zealand, and other parts of the southern hemisphere are dominated by eucalypts.

Mixed forests of deciduous and evergreen trees make up the third type of temperate forest. They are found in New England, the upper Midwest, northern and central Canada, and parts of the southeastern United States. They are also found in parts of Russia, northern Europe, and Asia. Due to their higher elevation, or more northern location, mixed forests are subject to long winters, lower average temperatures, and shorter growing seasons than are deciduous forests.

Those parts of the temperate zone closest to the equator may experience particularly heavy rainfall. As a result, forests in this area are often called temperate rainforests. They look very different from the deciduous forests of the north because their trees are mainly evergreen, remaining lush throughout the year. Bays, eucalypts, magnolias, evergreen oaks, and pine trees are typically found in these subtropical forests (forests bordering the tropical rainforest). Beneath these tall trees there is a mass of dense undergrowth, made up of creepers, ferns, and liverworts and mosses.

A layered environment

Temperate forests have distinct layers that dictate where different organisms can be found. The thick leaves of the tallest trees form the canopy layer. The canopy blocks sunlight, providing the forest's shady underlayers. It also catches rain, allowing the moisture to trickle to the ground below at a slow, even rate.

Beneath this is the understory, a layer made up of smaller tree species and shrubs, such as hawthorns, hazels, rhododendrons, and wild cherries. Only shade-tolerant trees can grow under the canopy. However, if a taller tree topples over, the gap in the canopy can be taken over by a tree from the understory, which is suddenly able to reach its full potential height as it strains to reach the sunlight.

▲ *This Great gray owl finds the temperate forest an ideal habitat in which to live. Given the number of small creatures, such as mice and voles, that live in the forest's ground cover, hunting is plentiful and success almost guaranteed.*

▶ *The Paper birch (Betula papyrifer) is a light-demanding species and an important colonist of forest clearings.*

Growing below the understory is yet another group of plants, which form the herb layer. The term "herb" is short for a herbaceous plant; that is, a plant that does not have a woody stem. Typical temperate forest herbs include ferns, grasses, and wildflowers. During the spring, when the leaves of the canopy have not yet grown back and the sun's rays can stream down to the ground, the herb layer may be alive with bright colors. At this time, carpets of pretty woodland flowers, such as bluebells, violets, and wood anemones, spread around the bases of the trees and shrubs. In newly created forest clearings, some herbs, such as foxgloves and goldenrods, quickly take advantage of the sunlight to sprout and flower.

Beneath the herb layer is the ground cover. This is made up of leaf and other plant litter, fungi, liverworts, and the remains of dead animals overlying the soil.

Creatures of the temperate forest

As you might expect from a habitat containing such a range of different plant species, temperate forests are home to a huge array of other organisms. Many of these creatures inhabit the soil and ground cover and are rarely seen by humans. Decomposers, such as fungi, insects, slugs, snails, and worms, are found in the soil. They are called decomposers because they break down the decaying plant and animal material, releasing the nutrients into the soil. Feeding on this rich source of energy are the small creatures of the forest, such as mice, shrews, and voles.

Many animals move between the ground and the tree canopy above. For example, Eastern chipmunks and Gray squirrels are often seen scampering around in the undergrowth and then racing up the tree trunks. Their favorite food items are berries, insects, nuts, and seeds.

A huge variety of birds also lives in the temperate zone, and the forests are usually alive with the sound of their songs. The prettiest songs come from the finches and warblers. Male robins sing particularly fiercely to defend their territory from their neighbors. Larger birds, such as crows and jays, are loud and raucous. In some forests, the Stellar's jay searches out the eggs and

KEY FACTS

● **Location**
Temperate forests are located in the temperate zone, between the taiga and the Tropic of Cancer in the northern hemisphere, and in Chile and New Zealand in the southern hemisphere

● **Climate**
Requires a minimum of four frost-free months and, on average, the rainfall is 75 to 250 cm (30 to 100 in), falling regularly throughout the year. In winter, the rain usually falls as snow

● **Typical plants**
Beeches, birches, bluebells, eucalypts, ferns, firs, grasses, hawthorns, hazels, hemlocks, hickories, larches, liverworts, maples, magnolias, mosses, oaks, pines, redwoods, spruces, violets, wood anemones

● **Typical animals**
Badgers, Brown creepers, chipmunks, deer, dormice, earthworms, foxes, Gray squirrels, hedgehogs, insects, jays, mice, nuthatches, owls, robins, slugs and snails, voles, Wild boar, woodpeckers,

nestlings of other bird species to eat. At night, a magical hooting sound can be heard through the trees as the hunters of the forest, the owls, prey on small, nocturnal rodents.

Several birds are well adapted to their life in temperate forests. Woodpeckers, for example, have specialized feet for clinging on to the trunks of trees. They have excellent hearing, too, which allows them to listen for insects moving around under the bark. You can often hear woodpeckers hammering away with their chisel-like beaks to get at the insects. They also use their sharp bills for drilling nesting chambers in the trees. Brown creepers and nuthatches also move up and down the trunks, looking for insects in the crevices of the bark. You can easily tell these two birds apart, as the Brown creeper always climbs upward from the base of the tree to the top of the trunk while the nuthatch creeps downward headfirst.

There are many large mammals to be found in temperate forests, too. If you were particularly quiet and patient, you might see herds of deer wandering through the trees and foxes slinking through the undergrowth. Badgers also make their homes here, digging a complex network of underground tunnels and chambers called a set. In each set there is usually a large social group of up to 12 animals, which venture out during the night to feed on fruits, leaves, and small animals such as insects and worms. In the temperate forests of Europe and Asia, relatives of the domestic farm pig, known as Wild boars, roam in search of fruits, nuts, and plant roots, which they dig up with their huge snouts. From time to time you might even see a large bear or a pack of wolves, although these animals are becoming rare inhabitants of temperate forests today.

Sleeping in winter

The annual leaf fall from broad-leaved trees means that deciduous forests are very different places in which to live throughout the seasons. In winter, the lack of overhead cover to shelter the inhabitants from the elements turns the temperate forest into a harsh environment.

In response, many animals, such as bears, dormice, hedgehogs, groundhogs, and fox squirrels, take the easy way out and hibernate until the warm weather and plentiful food return with the spring. Curled up into a tight ball, and snug in their nests or burrows, these animals are therefore able to save the energy that they would otherwise use up in keeping themselves warm.

◀ *The dormouse (Muscardinus avellanarius) adapts to the rhythms of the temperate forest. It eats well in the fall, when food is in abundance, and builds up its fat reserves for the winter. At this time, with little food available, it hibernates to conserve its energy in the cold.*

See also **Fungus, Larch, Liverwort, Oak, Pine, Rainforest**

Tenrec

Tenrecs are small insect-eating animals that have adapted to a wide variety of habitats and ways of life. There are 34 species altogether, most of them living on the island of Madagascar, with a few species found in central Africa. These animals range from water-dwelling otter-like shrews and burrowing mole-like animals with soft, velvety coats, to large, spiny, porcupine-like creatures.

Large, common, and tailless
The largest and heaviest of these animals is the Common, or Tailless, tenrec. Indeed, this animal is the largest living insectivore

(insect eater) in the world, growing up to 15 in (40 cm) from head to rump and weighing more than $4\frac{1}{2}$ lb (2 kg). The Common tenrec is closely related to the Lesser and Greater hedgehog tenrecs (*Echinops telfairi* and *Setifer setosus*), although its coat is slightly less spiny.

Common tenrecs are nocturnal animals (active at night). Their sight is poorly developed, and they rely more on their acute senses of hearing and smell when searching for food in the dark undergrowth. Foraging through the leaf litter on the forest floor with their snouts close to the ground, Common tenrecs eat

▼ *Unlike its cousin the tree-climbing Lesser hedgehog tenrec, the Common tenrec (shown here) has only very short limbs and almost no visible tail to help it balance, and it is strictly a ground-dwelling animal.*

vegetation and fruit, or prey on insects and other invertebrates such as earthworms. However, they also catch and eat small vertebrates such as reptiles, amphibians, birds, and small mammals.

A large family

Common tenrecs breed during the wet season in October and November, when there are large numbers of invertebrates for them to eat. About two months after mating, the female gives birth to a large litter of up to 32 young! She has up to 29 nipples from which to suckle her offspring – the most recorded in any mammal. Because of the huge amount of milk that she needs to provide for this number of babies, a Common tenrec mother is forced to forage for food during the day as well as at night.

As they get older and are weaned by about seven weeks old, the young

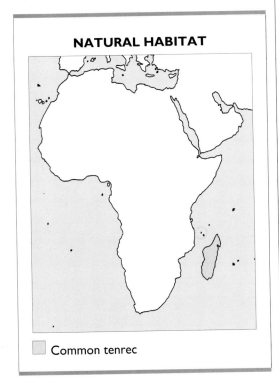

NATURAL HABITAT

Common tenrec

▲ As its name suggests, the Lesser hedgehog tenrec (**Echinops telfairi**) *looks like a European hedgehog, with sharp spines covering its body. If it is disturbed, it may roll itself into a prickly ball.*

accompany their mother during the day and have striped coats to camouflage them against daytime predators. This patterning fades as they become adult. The young tenrecs communicate with their mother by smell and sound. When faced with danger they signal alarm by rubbing together the spines on their backs to make a loud noise. This technique is called stridulation.

Aggressive defense

If disturbed, the Common tenrec can be extremely aggressive. Unlike some of its relatives that immediately take flight or roll themselves up into a spiny ball for protection, it actually moves toward its enemy, hissing with its powerful jaws gaping wide and its head swinging from side to side. If the sight of the large, sharp teeth does not scare away the predator or intruder, the tenrec's head-swinging tactics may cause special detachable spines in its neck to become lodged painfully in the intruder's body.

KEY FACTS

● **Name**
Common or Tailless tenrec (*Tenrec ecaudatus*)

● **Range**
Madagascar and nearby islands, including Comoro

● **Habitat**
Forests: especially tropical rainforests

● **Appearance**
Large shrew-like animal, measuring 10½-15 in (26.5-40 cm); males are much larger than females; the reddish-brown coat is thin and rough to the touch, interspersed with long, almost spiky, black hairs; a long, pointed snout and short limbs

● **Food**
Earthworms, insects and their larvae; occasionally small vertebrates; plant material

● **Breeding**
Breeding occurs Oct-Nov; a litter of 16-32 (usually about 15) is born about 2 months after mating; the young are weaned at about 1½ months old

● **Status**
Common

See also **Hedgehog**

919

Termite

▲ Termite mounds are giant fortresses built from termite feces mixed with saliva, which sets as hard as cement when it dries. Some mounds may reach heights of 18 ft (5.4 m) or more.

Termites are what scientists call social insects that live and work together in large colonies. Within these colonies, termites are divided into castes (groups), with each group carrying out its own specific tasks. Another group of insects that has very similar cooperative behavior is ants, although ants and termites do not look alike and are not related. Termites are fairly basic insects that are related to cockroaches, while ants are closely related to bees and wasps.

Termites are mainly found in the warmer regions of the world, including Australia and Africa, and in some parts of the United States. There are about 2000 species divided into seven families. The true termites make up the largest family (the *Termitidae*), which contains about three quarters of all the termite species.

Termite fortresses

Termites construct their nests in soil or wood, and some species build huge mounds above ground, cemented together with a mixture of feces and saliva. In parts of Africa and Australia there may be hundreds of these giant fortresses in an area, with each nest containing thousands, or even a million, termites. All the termites that live in the nest are the offspring of the king and queen that founded the colony. The king and queen are known as the primary reproducers, because they are usually the only members of the colony that breed. They spend their lives in a special chamber, where they are looked after by the workers. The king, who is about the size of a wasp, has only one function: to fertilize the queen's eggs. The queen is a grossly overgrown egg producer that grows to a length of 4¾ in (12 cm) and looks very much like a fat, white sausage. She produces up to 30,000 eggs in one day, most of which will hatch into worker or soldier termites.

Caring for the colony

Both male and female termites function as workers and soldiers, but they are sterile (they cannot reproduce). Each type of termite has clearly defined jobs to do in the colony, and to some extent this is reflected in their appearance.

The workers are usually small, blind, and wingless. They build and maintain the nest, care for the eggs and young, forage for food, and feed all the other members of the colony. The soldiers, on the other hand, have large heads, with huge, powerful jaws, and their main duty is to guard and protect the colony from intruders – particularly from ants, the termites' main enemies. Like the workers, soldiers are also wingless.

In addition to workers and soldiers, there may be another small group of wingless termites known as secondary reproductives, which can take over the role of king or queen if one of these "royal" termites dies.

When the workers locate a source of food, they chew it and then pass it on to

NATURAL HABITAT

▲ *These worker Harvester termites in Transvaal, South Africa, are repairing a hole in the wall of their nest while soldiers stand guard.*

the others by mouth-to-mouth feeding. This type of feeding enables termites to transmit chemical messages to each other. The messages are present in the saliva and feces and tell the other termites about their surroundings.

Living on wood

Wood-boring termites that live in trees and wooden buildings have specially developed microorganisms in their bodies that enable them to digest the wood. Other termites eat a variety of living and decaying vegetable matter, including leaves and grasses. Some termites, such as the macrotermes of Australia for example, also feed on fungi that they cultivate in underground chambers.

☐ Harvester termite

KEY FACTS

● **Name**
Harvester termite (*Hodotermitidae*, a family of 17 species)

● **Range**
Africa, Arabia, Asia

● **Habitat**
Dry grasslands

● **Appearance**
Small golden-brown insects, workers growing up to 0.3 in (8 mm) and queens up to 1 in (25 mm); reproductives have 2 pairs of temporary wings, but workers and soldiers are wingless; 6 legs and a head with biting mouthparts

● **Food**
Grass

● **Breeding**
Only the king and queen of the colony breed; several times a year the queen lays hundreds of eggs that hatch into winged males and females; these fly away in pairs to found new colonies; each queen then produces about 30,000 eggs a day, which hatch into sterile workers and soldiers

● **Status**
Common and widespread

See also **Ant, Cockroach, Grassland**

Tern

Terns are graceful and agile sea birds that belong to the same family as gulls. Most species live along the coasts or above the open ocean, but some species are found up rivers or on inland marshes. One species of tern, the Arctic tern, has the longest migration route of any bird.

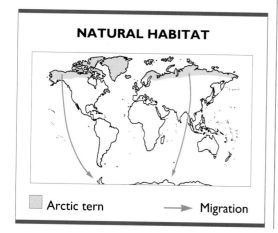

NATURAL HABITAT

Arctic tern   ⟶ Migration

Long distance travelers

Terns are the masters of the air, spending hours, days, and sometimes years on end in flight. The Sooty tern (*Sterna fuscata*) is renowned for its flying ability: from the time that it leaves its nest until the time when it is ready to breed three or four years later, it never settles on land or water. It is even able to sleep while it flies! Many species are migratory, moving to warmer parts of the world when the winter arrives in the northern hemisphere. Arctic terns, for example, travel all the way from the Arctic Circle to the Antarctic and back every year without stopping, feeding by diving for fish along the way. They get more sunlight per year than any other creature. At each end of

▲ Although they spend most of their lives far out at sea, these Sooty terns gather in vast colonies to breed. They are found on islands and remote coasts around tropical seas during the breeding season.

▶ Arctic terns travel farther than any other bird in their migration. Each way they make a journey of about 11,000 miles (18,000 km).

their journey they can take advantage of the rich food supply that exists there for only half the year. Other North American species are less energetic, moving only from Canada to the southern states for the winter. Some species live in tropical regions and do not migrate at all.

To help with their flight, many species of tern have long, forked tails, rather like those of swallows. Most terns have predominantly white or white and gray coloring, often with black feathers on their heads. Their legs and feet, and their sharp, pointed beaks come in a variety of colors.

Diving for food

Terns feed mainly on fish, crustaceans, and squid. Although they have webbed feet, which are helpful for swimming, their legs are short and not very muscular, so they rarely settle on the water when they are hunting. Instead they hover over the sea in search of prey, and then plunge headlong beneath the surface of the water in order to catch it.

Terns use their flight as part of their courtship display, soaring upward with forked tails spread out. In many species the male brings gifts of food to his mate, and he often struts up and down the breeding ground with his feathers held erect. These breeding grounds are usually on islands or in very remote areas where there are few predators to attack the nests. Terns nest in large colonies, so if a predator does approach, only one bird has to spot it and it can warn all the other birds. Terns' nests are very basic, no more than a scrape on the ground lined with grass. The pretty White tern (*Gygis alba*) of tropical seas simply deposits its single egg on the branch of a tree or a ledge on a cliff – it makes no nest at all.

Both parents work to feed and protect their young, attacking any intruders and catching small fish to feed them. When they first hatch, the young birds are mottled and speckled in tones of brown. This helps to camouflage them against predators such as skuas and birds of prey.

KEY FACTS

- **Name**
  Arctic tern
  (*Sterna paradisaea*)

- **Range**
  All around the world in the Arctic, moving to sub-Antarctic and Antarctic seas during the winter in the northern hemisphere

- **Habitat**
  Open ocean

- **Appearance**
  13-15 in (33-38 cm) long; white underneath, a gray back and black cap; a red beak and legs

- **Food**
  Crustaceans and small fish

- **Breeding**
  Arctic terns breed farther north than any other bird; they nest in colonies on the bare ground of beaches, islands, sand bars, or wet tundra; they scrape out a hollow and line it with grass; 2-3 eggs are incubated for about 3 weeks by both parents; the parents feed the young with small fish

- **Status**
  Widespread, but faces the threat of pollution and toxic wastes

See also **Gull, Skua**

Terrapin

The terrapin is a four-legged reptile with a hard, bony shell on the upper and lower surfaces of its body. It is closely related to the tortoises and turtles, and together these three make up the group of reptiles known as the chelonians or testudines.

Terrapin or turtle?
In the United States, scientists use the word "terrapin" to refer to one particular species, the Diamond-back terrapin. However, the early European settlers of North America used the word to describe any edible turtle found in water. Even today the name terrapin is sometimes used for a small number of freshwater turtles such as the Geographic or Map terrapin (*Graptemys geographica*) that lives in the waters of the St Lawrence and Missouri

rivers and in the Great Lakes. In Europe almost any small turtle that lives both on land and in freshwater is called a terrapin.

The Diamond-back terrapin is found from New England to the Gulf of Mexico. It is much more aquatic (water-dwelling) than the freshwater turtles, and is always found in or near water in salt marshes, estuaries, the sea, and in rivers as far upstream as the tide reaches. The Diamond-back appears to need salty water to prevent fungi from growing on its shell; when it has been kept as a pet in freshwater these growths appear, but they disappear soon after salt has been added to the aquarium water.

Like most of its cousins, the Diamond-back's carapace (upper shell) is rather flattened; by contrast, in land-dwelling

KEY FACTS

- **Name**
  Diamond-back terrapin (*Malaclemys terrapin*)

- **Range**
  Massachusetts to Florida, Texas, and Mexico

- **Habitat**
  Salt water, on and near the coast

- **Appearance**
  Males grow up to 6 in (15 cm) long and females 8 in (20 cm); a greenish-brown carapace (upper shell), with dark, diamond-shaped or circular lines; the plastron (lower shell) and sides are yellow

- **Food**
  Crustaceans, insects

- **Breeding**
  4-18 eggs laid in the spring, which hatch in about 3 months

- **Status**
  Rare

◀ *This European pond terrapin is completely carnivorous (meat eating) and feeds on snails, frogs, and fish.*

tortoises the carapace is usually highly arched. The Diamond-back's shell is greenish-brown with dark, diamond-shaped or circular markings. Its plastron (lower shell), however, is yellowish with dark spots and the skin is pale and marked with dark specks. The male Diamond-back is smaller than the female, measuring about 6 in (15 cm) in length; the female is 8 in (20 cm) long.

Water baby

The Diamond-back terrapin spends much of its time swimming and hunting for food. The bulk of its diet is made up of small water-dwelling animals such as Fiddler crabs and periwinkles as well as insects and their larvae, although it also feeds on many types of plant material.

When this terrapin rests it either crawls out of the water and basks on a rock, or floats near the surface with its body almost vertical in the water and only its snout showing above the surface. It uses its small webbed feet to steady itself when it is floating and to move through the water when it is swimming.

In the fall the Diamond-back burrows into the mud and hibernates for the winter. Shortly after it emerges in the spring it looks for a mate. Eggs may be laid in May or as late as the end of June, depending on where the terrapin lives. The female makes a nest on land and lays between 4 and 18 white oval eggs. Older females lay up to two clutches a year, but younger ones may lay only one.

A dish of terrapin

People have had a taste for eating turtles for centuries, and they have long been the main ingredient in turtle soup, as well as a basic foodstuff for many people. In the late eighteenth century, terrapins were also eaten by poorer people in North America, but later became fashionable among the rich as terrapin stew. The Diamondback's popularity as an item on the menu contributed to its falling numbers in the nineteenth century, and now it is legally protected in most states.

▲ *The Diamond-back terrapin gets its name from the ridges on its carapace, or upper shell, which form diamond-like shapes or circles. This species is the only North American terrapin to be adapted for a life mainly spent in salt water.*

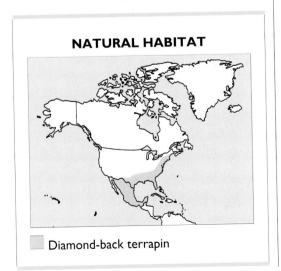

NATURAL HABITAT

Diamond-back terrapin

See also **Lake, river, and estuary; Tortoise; Turtle**

Tide pool and coast

A coastline is the meeting point of the land and the ocean. In some coasts, sandy beaches may border the ocean. In other places, rocks form a shoreline, which is pounded by the often violent seas.

Highs and lows

Gravity keeps the water in the oceans, but it is the gravitational pull of the moon and the sun that creates the tides. In certain positions, the moon and sun exert a strong pull on the oceans, which rise up toward them, causing a high tide. In other positions, this pull has less effect and the waters settle down into a low tide.

Life on rocky shores

Rocky coastlines can be divided into a number of regions. The point farthest from the water is called the splash zone. This area is home to alga, marine lichens, limpets, and periwinkles, which are often splashed by the ocean spray and by rain. These organisms have adapted to survive in the exposed conditions of the splash zone. For example, algae are covered with a slimy substance that prevents them from drying out during periods when they are exposed to the sun.

The high intertidal zone lies just below the splash zone. This area is covered by sea water only 10 percent of the time, when the ocean waves regularly crash into the rocks. Despite this, rock barnacles, rockweed (*Fucus sargassum*), and shore crabs can live here. All these organisms produce glue-like substances that allow

them to stick to the rocks and prevent them from being washed away.

Further toward the sea lies the middle intertidal zone. This area is covered with water during high tide and exposed to the air during low tide. Organisms in this zone must be able to survive extremely variable conditions. In the lower, wetter sections of the zone, Irish moss (*Chondrus crispus*) and Sea lettuce (*Ulva lactuca*) thrive. Countless tiny animals, such as tube worms and ribbon worms, live among, or attached to, these plants.

Blue mussels (*Mytilus edulis*) live in colonies attached to middle-intertidal rocks, as do masses of barnacles. During high tide, the barnacles' shells open, revealing their feathery arms (tentacles), which trap minute particles of food floating in the water. During low tide, the shells shut tight to avoid loss of water (dehydration).

▲ *This coastal landscape has been shaped by the sea. It continually changes, subject as it is to the ebb and flow of the tides and the relentless pounding of the ocean waves.*

The low intertidal zone is almost always covered by seawater. Various species of kelp and other seaweeds live in the low intertidal zone, as do sea anemones, sea stars, sea urchins, and sponges. Of all the zones, this area is the one richest in life.

Sandy shores

Sand is fine particles of rock pulverized by the action of waves. Sand can come from the seafloor. The silty particles are washed onto the shore at high tide. On some beaches, sand is largely the ground shells and remains of dead organisms.

Sandy shorelines can also be divided into zones, but the lack of rocks limits the variety of organisms. Many of the animals that live in the sand are burrowing organisms such as clams, cockles, crabs, shrimp, and worms. All these creatures are well adapted to a life beneath the sand. For example, mollusks have siphons that stick out of the sand so that they can suck in food particles when sea water washes over them. The siphons also suck in sand particles. When the particle mix reaches the mollusks' feeding organs (gills) the food particles are absorbed. However, the gills filter out the sand particles, which are ejected back through the siphon.

Tide pools

Tide pools are little habitats of their own, the life-giving water replenished at nearly every high tide. Those in the middle intertidal zone are like aquariums, teeming with the life brought in by the sea.

The bottom of a tide pool is covered with silt. Tiny saltwater plants take root and form miniature forests. Minute algae

and near-invisible marine animals teem in the water. Snails and shrimp are common, as are small sea anemones and hydroids. Small fish, such as the sculpin, may be tossed by a wave into a tide pool and live by feeding on the tiny worms there.

Deep pools are better able to maintain a stable water temperature than shallow pools, whose waters heat up quickly. Thus, as the salt water in a shallow tide pool heats, it begins to evaporate; the remaining water contains a higher concentration of salt. To survive, organisms living in such shallow tide pools must be able to adapt to these extreme changes in salt concentration and temperature.

Pollution is another threat to organisms that live in tide pools and coastal habitats. Pollution may result from oil and chemical spillages, sewage, pesticides, or plastic waste. It may contaminate the sea directly or indirectly from the rivers or rainfall.

▼ *These Gooseneck barnacles are attached to a fishing float. Barnacles use their feathery arms (tentacles) to trap food particles in the sea.*

See also **Alga, Crab, Kelp and other seaweeds, Ocean, Sea anemone**

Tiger

With its distinctive black-striped, reddish-gold coat, the tiger is one of the most recognizable animals in the world. The largest of the big cats (a group of animals that includes the lion, leopard, and jaguar), it may grow to over 12 ft (3.5 m) long from its head to the tip of its tail, and weigh as much as 660 lb (300 kg).

This magnificent cat has long been the focus of human's fear and respect: it has a powerful, muscular body, loud roar, and frightening snarl revealing large, sharp

▼ *Tigers are excellent swimmers and some, such as this Sumatran subspecies (Panthera tigris sumatrae), often enter water in order to cool off in the intense heat of their tropical habitats.*

teeth. Unlike their close cousins the lions, tigers are solitary creatures that spend all their time alone. Each tiger has its own territory, which it advertises to intruders by scratching the bark of trees, spraying urine, and leaving piles of feces. Males are particularly aggressive toward other male neighbors, although their home ranges may contain those of two or three females. Tigers' territories are usually very large, and in the case of males they extend to over 40 sq miles (100 km²).

A stealthy predator

The tiger is a nocturnal animal (active at night) and prefers to hunt its food under the cover of dense vegetation. It hunts by stealth, stalking its prey silently through the trees in a low crouch until it is within 66 ft (20 m). Then it bounds forward, knocking its victim over with a swipe of its huge forepaw and pouncing upon its back as it falls to the ground. The tiger kills small prey by a single bite to the back of the neck with its large, powerful jaws and sharp teeth. It deals with larger prey by getting a suffocating grip on the throat.

Once it has made a kill, the tiger usually drags the carcass under cover before beginning to feed. Then it starts to eat from the rump, guarding its meal jealously and making loud growling and snarling noises as a warning to other predators in the area. Tigers need to eat about 40 lb (18 kg) of meat a day and will commonly cover up to 12 miles (20 km) every night in search of suitable prey. This is usually

◄ *This tigress is carrying one of her cubs, gripping it by the scruff of the neck.*

KEY FACTS

● **Name**
Tiger (*Panthera tigris*)

● **Range**
India, Manchuria, China, Indonesia

● **Habitat**
Most forest types, including rainforests

● **Appearance**
12 ft (3.5 m) from head to tail; the coat is reddish-gold with black stripes, the markings varying among subspecies; whitish underparts and white around the face

● **Food**
Mainly large hoofed mammals; also small mammals and some livestock

● **Breeding**
Female gives birth to a litter of 3-4 cubs, which are born blind and helpless; the cubs are weaned at 5-6 months and leave their mother's range when they are about 2¹/₂ years old

● **Status**
Endangered

large hoofed mammals, such as sambars, elk, and buffalo, as well as young rhinos and elephants.

Once tigers have reached the age of three or four years they are old enough to breed. Just over three months after mating, the female gives birth to a litter of three to four cubs in a special den. These cubs are blind and helpless at first, and the mother rears them alone, with no help from the father. She suckles them until they are five to six weeks old. Soon they are able to go on hunting trips with her, learning skills that they will need later to survive on their own.

An endangered species

There were originally eight subspecies of tiger, differing mainly in coat pattern. Once widespread throughout Asia, three subspecies are now probably extinct, and the remaining ones are endangered as a result of the loss of suitable habitat and decreasing numbers of prey.

NATURAL HABITAT

Tiger

929

Toad

The common American toad lives a quiet, almost secretive life in damp habitats, hiding under logs or in reeds, ready to plop into the water to escape predators or catch its prey. It is very similar to the common American bullfrog. Both species vary in color, but the toad is usually reddish-brown, while the bullfrog is more often green. The toad is smaller and rounder than the bullfrog, but it is less agile and has to hop rather than leap from danger. It is active mainly at night.

Scientists classify these two amphibians in different groups, but some frogs and toads are closely related and there are no precise definitions to distinguish them.

Breeding similarities

The American toad also has a similar life cycle and breeding technique to the American frog. It mates in the water, with the male attracting his mate with a distinctive croaking call. He amplifies the call by puffing up his throat. The female lays eggs that are protected by a layer of jelly while the male grips her from behind, ready to fertilize them in the water. However, the toad lays strings of eggs while the frog lays her eggs in a large mass. The eggs hatch into tadpoles that slowly metamorphose (change) as they grow. The tails gradually shrink away as the tadpoles grow legs.

KEY FACTS

● **Name**
American toad (*Bufo americanus*)

● **Range**
Southeastern Canada to the southern U.S.

● **Habitat**
Under leaves, logs, or in the ground

● **Appearance**
2-4½ in (5-11 cm); reddish-brown to gray, with a rounded body and a flat head

● **Food**
Insects and other small invertebrates

● **Breeding**
Mate in the spring in ponds or streams; the female lays a string of eggs that are fertilized by the male as they leave her body; tadpoles hatch a week later and take 2 months to develop into toadlets

● **Status**
Common

◀ *The male American toad puffs up his throat when he gives his mating call to amplify the sound.*

930

Many other toads are found in North America that belong to the same family as the American toad. These include the Great plains toad (*Bufo cognatus*), the Houston toad (*Bufo Houstonensis*), which is endangered, and the Giant marine toad (*Bufo marinus*), one of the largest toads in the world. However, some toads in the same family have quite different breeding habits. The female West African live-bearing toad (*Nectophrynoides occidentalis*), for example, holds her eggs in a pocket inside her body after they have been fertilized. The baby toads develop through the tadpole stage while they are still inside the jelly that surrounded the eggs, so that tiny toadlets are "borne" by the mother.

Many relations

There are many other toads, living in many different habitats. Some toads, including the brightly colored Burrowing toad (*Rhinophrynus dorsalis*) and the spadefoot toads of the southern states, live in near-desert conditions. They keep themselves moist and cool by burrowing into the ground, and they rely on sudden,

NATURAL HABITAT

American toad

heavy showers for pools and puddles where they can breed.

The Surinam toad (*Pipa pipa*) of South America has an unusual way of protecting its eggs. After the female has laid her eggs and the male has fertilized them, they are maneuvered into pockets on the back of the female. Here the eggs hatch and the tadpoles develop, each in a separate pocket. Midwife toads have special egg-care arrangements because the adults spend almost all the time out of the water.

▲ *In the Common midwife toad (Alytes obstetricans) of Europe (above), the strings of eggs laid by the female are wrapped around the male's legs. When they are ready to hatch he takes them to water so the tadpoles can swim away.*

See also **Frog**

Tomato

When tomatoes were first introduced to Europe in the sixteenth century, only the bravest souls dared attempt to eat them. Even though the Spanish brought them from Mexico, where they were already cultivated as a food crop, they were suspected of being poisonous, so cooks carefully boiled them for at least three hours before eating them. With such an unpromising start, it's a wonder that this marvelous fruit became the staple of European cooking it is today, especially in Italy.

What's in a name?

When it first reached Europe, the tomato was called *pomodoro,* meaning "golden apple." This has led historians to suggest that the original tomatoes were yellow. Tomatoes are native mainly to Ecuador and Peru. They were cultivated in ancient Mexico, and their modern name comes from the Aztec word *tomatl.*

Deadly plant, delicious fruit

All parts of the tomato plant, except the fruit, contain poison. Most plants in the *Solanaceae* family contain toxins. Deadly nightshade and jimsonweed are examples of poisonous plants in this family. The

▲ *Bright red tomatoes, ripe to bursting, are an essential ingredient of summer salads.*

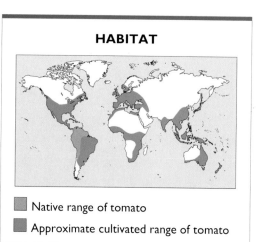

HABITAT

☐ Native range of tomato

■ Approximate cultivated range of tomato

potato plant is another member and contains poison in all parts except for its root growths (the familiar potatoes we love to eat). The eggplant is closely related to the tomato, but here again a plant that is largely toxic provides us with delicious food.

Tomatoes are classified in the same group (genus) as potatoes (*Solanum* spp.). The tomatoes we eat today are varieties of *Solanum lycopersicum*. Most tomato plants sprawl along the ground as the fruit matures. Gardeners with little growing space often use sticks to keep them upright. Cherry tomato plants and dwarf varieties are usually compact and bushy and need no support. Varieties such as beefsteak tomato or other slicing or sauce tomatoes will grow up to 6½ ft (2 m) tall.

Tomato plants have many branches. Fruit yields are improved if secondary branches, or shoots, that grow from the crooks of main branches are pinched off. The leaves of tomato plants are compound (meaning they are made up of several leaflets). They can grow to 12 in (30 cm) long and may have rolled edges. The whole plant is hairy and aromatic.

The small, yellow flowers of *Solanum lycopersicum* grow in clusters. In the cultivated varieties they usually self-pollinate, needing no help from insects. Once they are pollinated they begin to set seed and develop their fruit – the tomato.

Tomatoes are soft, sweet to tangy berries (fruits that are made up of several seeds surrounded by flesh). Tomato seeds are set in a jelly-like substance called the pulp. The pulp, which contains a large amount of vitamin C, is surrounded by the fruit's tasty flesh.

Countless varieties

It was only in the early twentieth century that tomatoes truly became popular. At this time, varieties suitable for different uses (sauces or raw in salads) and different climates (tropical or temperate regions) were developed.

The most popular kinds of tomatoes are the large, round, sweet, and juicy beefsteak

▶ *Tomatoes are at first green, ripening rapidly through yellow and orange to glossy red. Green tomatoes can be used for jam.*

tomatoes people grow in their gardens and cut up to eat raw in summer salads. Other widely grown tomatoes include the oval or pear-shaped plum tomatoes used in tomato sauces and the bite-size delectable morsels known as cherry tomatoes. Though most tomatoes we eat are bright red, some tomato varieties may produce yellow fruits.

A global fruit

Tomatoes originated in the tropics and subtropics, near the Andes Mountains in South America. Their current popularity among people around the world has led to varieties specific for other climates. Some varieties are more cold-tolerant and grow better in the United States, Canada, and northern Europe. Even so, no tomato plant can tolerate frost. The seeds of temperate-climate tomatoes must be started indoors or in greenhouses. Tiny seedlings can be planted outdoors in the garden when the danger of frost has passed. Wherever they grow, tomatoes need fertile soil, good rainfall, warm weather, and lots of sunlight.

See also **Deadly nightshade, Potato**

Tortoise

Some of the longest-living animals in the world, tortoises are wrinkled, ancient-looking reptiles with large, patterned shells. There are over 40 different species of tortoise, belonging to the group of reptiles known as the chelonians or testudines. In some ways it is difficult to distinguish between the tortoises and their close cousins the turtles and terrapins, but in general turtles and terrapins are largely aquatic (water-dwelling) animals, while the tortoises live entirely on land.

Tortoises are found in many of the world's tropical and subtropical regions, although most species are found in Africa and Madagascar. The largest species are the giant tortoises of the Galapagos Islands in the Pacific Ocean and those found on a few islands in the Indian Ocean.

There are four species of tortoise found in North America. These are known as gopher tortoises. They live in wooded or sandy areas (two occur in deserts and semideserts), mainly in the southern states and also in Mexico, where they burrow into the earth and live underground.

A burrowing lifestyle

Like other tortoises, turtles, and terrapins, gopher tortoises have large shells covering their bodies, consisting of a carapace (upper shell) and a plastron (lower shell). However, their shells have a special adaptation to a burrowing lifestyle. The front of the plastron extends outward at the front beneath the throat to form a broad "shovel" with which the tortoises can dig their underground chambers.

KEY FACTS

- **Name**
  Gopher tortoise (*Gopherus polyphemus*)

- **Range**
  Southern U.S., Mexico

- **Habitat**
  Sandy and wooded regions

- **Appearance**
  $9\frac{1}{4}$-$14\frac{1}{2}$ in (23.5-37 cm) long; a domed shell; scaly, flattened forelegs for digging

- **Food**
  Grass, leaves, fruit, seedlings

- **Breeding**
  Mate in spring; the female lays several clutches, each containing 2-7 eggs, in a shallow pit from April-July

- **Status**
  Threatened

◄ *Gopher tortoises, like gophers, spend much of their time in underground burrows, which is how they got their common name.*

The gopher species and other small tortoises, which have shells from about 8-24 in (20-60 cm) long, were once very popular as pets and were often let outside during the summer. As a result, many people know them as "garden" tortoises.

Despite a marked difference in size, the garden tortoises have many characteristics in common with the giant species. There are five unwebbed toes on each of the short front feet and four on the back, each toe ending in a sharp claw. The carapace has a high dome and, with the plastron, forms a bony "box" into which the scaly head, limbs, and tail can be completely withdrawn when the tortoise is disturbed.

Tortoises are vegetarians that feed on a variety of plant food such as seedlings, fruit, and leaves. They also occasionally eat insects. Tortoises living in temperate climates stop feeding in the fall, and several weeks later dig themselves into the earth or under dead vegetation to hibernate for the winter.

In the spring or summer, the female lays her eggs (up to 50 in some species) in a hole she has dug in the ground. She covers up the eggs, but leaves them to incubate and hatch on their own. The young tortoises emerge four months later.

The brink of extinction

The stock of giant tortoises has been heavily depleted, both on the Galápagos Islands and in the Indian Ocean. When sailing ships traveled the trade routes between Europe and Asia, and between Europe and North and South America, the sailors caught many of the tortoises for food. The number of giant tortoises also

fell dramatically because of loss of habitat and, especially in the Galápagos, from the deliberate introduction of domestic animals and the accidental introduction of rats. Rats and pigs killed young tortoises and also ate their eggs, while goats and other domestic animals competed with the tortoises for food. Today the Galápagos Giant tortoise is protected but still endangered. Of the many individuals that once lived on the islands of the Indian Ocean, all are extinct in the wild except for a few on South Aldabra Island.

NATURAL HABITAT

◻ Gopher tortoise

▲ *These Giant tortoises (Testudo elephantopus) live on the Galápagos Islands in the Pacific Ocean. These are the largest of all the terrapins, turtles, and tortoises. One Giant tortoise kept in captivity had a shell measuring 4 ft (1.3 m) in length and weighed 300 lb (140 kg). Another, living on the Galápagos island of Santa Cruz, weighed about 396 lb (180 kg). These tortoises are also extremely long-lived; one lived for at least 152 years. The record only began when the tortoise was already fully grown!*

See also **Terrapin, Turtle**

Toucan

The 41 species of toucans, aracaris, and toucanets are members of the family *Ramphastidae*. They live in the rainforests and woodlands of tropical Central and South America. They are best known for their enormous, often brightly colored, bills; in some species the bill is as long and as big as the bird's body. But although these bills are large, they are very light: they are almost hollow inside, held together by a network of bony fibers.

Reaching for food

The toucan's long bill enables it to reach out and take berries and fruit from branches that are too thin for it to stand on, and because the bill is so light the bird does not run the risk of tipping over while

▲ *The bill of the Toco toucan is very colorful. It may measure up to 8 in (20 cm), while the bird itself is only 26 in (66 cm) including its bill.*

doing so. The bill is also strong enough to to take eggs and nestlings from the nests of other birds. Other food includes insects and spiders, and even small reptiles and amphibians. The toucan seizes its food with the tip of the bill, and then tosses its head up to throw the food into its throat. Its tongue, which is long, narrow, and flattened, is almost as long as its bill.

All the colors of the rainbow, with the exception of violet, are found in the bills of different toucan species. The varied patterns and colors help individuals to recognize one another, and play a part in courtship. The bills do not usually differ between sexes, but males' are often larger.

Nesting high

Toucans build their nests in holes high in the trees, but their beaks are not strong enough to drill holes for themselves, so they sometimes drive out woodpeckers and take over their nests. They make no lining for the nest, but the floor frequently becomes covered with seeds from the fruit

NATURAL HABITAT

Toco toucan

▶ *Toucans spend most of their time high in the treetops, hopping from branch to branch or taking short flights from one tree to another, and rarely descend to the ground. They even bathe in pools of rainwater that have gathered in hollows between the branches.*

they have eaten. Two to four white eggs are laid, and both parents sit on them for about 16 days. When they hatch, the young are blind and naked, and develop feathers very slowly. Both parents feed their young with partly digested fruit, and the nestlings are fledged at 6-7 weeks.

Noisy croaks

Toucans are sociable birds. They form loose flocks, especially where the trees are heavy with fruit, but they do not move together like some other birds. One will fly to another tree, and a second follows, then a third, and a fourth, until eventually they have all moved. Their calls are unmusical harsh croaks, barks, and rattles.

Toucans are divided into four groups. The biggest belong to the group *Ramphastos* – 11 species including the Toco toucan – and have mainly black feathers. The 13 species of aracari are also mostly black, but smaller and more slender. The toucanets are smaller still. Some live high in the mountains and are mostly green in color, others live in tropical forests and have patterned feathers. The Saffron toucanet (*Baillonius bailloni*) is found in southeastern Brazil. The Mountain toucans also live at high altitudes.

Many toucans are becoming rare as their habitats are destroyed. The Yellow-browed toucanet (*Aulacorhynchus huallagae*) of Peru is listed as rare, almost threatened.

KEY FACTS

- **Name**
  Toco toucan
  (*Ramphastos toco*)

- **Range**
  Guianas, eastern Brazil, Paraguay, northern Argentina, and northern Bolivia

- **Habitat**
  Forests and woodlands

- **Appearance**
  Length (including bill) 26 in (66 cm); the male has the biggest bill of any toucan: 8 in (20 cm) long; mostly black, with white at the throat and the base of the tail; the underside of the tail is red; yellow skin around each eye; a yellow-orange bill with a black tip; blue feet

- **Food**
  Mainly fruit, but also the eggs and young of other birds

- **Breeding**
  Builds nest in a hollow tree; lays 2 eggs; parents feed their young on fruit and insects, but they develop very slowly and cannot leave the nest until about 50 days after hatching

- **Status**
  Common

Tree kangaroo

There are six species of tree kangaroo. As their name suggests, they spend most of their time unlike other kangaroos, high among the branches of the rainforests of northeastern Australia and New Guinea. Scientists believe that all kangaroos originally lived in trees, and that the giant ground-living "roos," with their large hind legs for hopping, developed from them.

Balancing act

With tails as long as their bodies, or even longer, tree kangaroos were often mistaken for monkeys by the first Europeans who saw them. They have long, strong forelegs, almost as large as their hind legs, and can leap from branch to branch over distances as far as 30 ft (9 m).

Although they have long, curved claws for gripping tree trunks and branches, tree kangaroos climb very clumsily. They usually descend tree trunks backward,

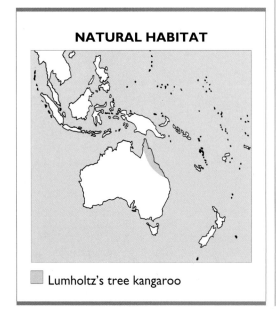

NATURAL HABITAT

Lumholtz's tree kangaroo

▲ *Sitting high in the trees like a small monkey, this Lumholtz's tree kangaroo (Dendrolagus lumholtzi) is easily recognizable by its very dark, almost black, face. These animals are very shy and secretive, spending most of their time alone rather than in large groups.*

clinging on with all four clawed feet, but if they are disturbed they can leap to the ground from as high as 60 ft (18 m) without injuring themselves.

Tree kangaroos spend most of the day asleep in a high tree fork, waking occasionally to browse on nearby leaves. At night they often come down from the trees to feed on leaves and fruit, holding the fruit or branch between their forepaws as they eat. On the ground they move by hopping, like other kangaroos, but have to lean forward to balance their long tails.

Depending on the species, the head and body of a tree kangaroo may be 19-32 in (48-81 cm) in length with a tail of 16½-37 in (42-94 cm), and the males are generally larger than the females. Their hair is long and soft, and may be black, brown, or gray, with a dark face and a much paler belly. When the animal is curled up asleep in the fork of a tree, the hair on its back points in all directions so that any rain runs straight off.

Secretive marsupials

Tree kangaroos live alone, although a male may have a harem of several females. Like other kangaroos they are marsupial, and the female has a well-developed pouch in which she raises a single young. Because they live deep in the rainforest mountains, as high as 10,000 ft (3000 m), and because they are shy and solitary creatures that spend their days in the upper branches of the trees, very little is known about their breeding habits. They do not appear to have a fixed breeding season, and nothing is known about how long the baby takes to develop inside its mother;

nor is it known how long the offspring spends in its mother's pouch before it is weaned, or whether, like kangaroos, the mother mates again as soon as it is born.

Clearing forests

All six species of tree kangaroo are threatened by the clearance of the rainforests, particularly in northern Queensland, and they are also hunted in New Guinea. Five species are now rare, but Lumholtz's tree kangaroo is still fairly common in those parts of the Queensland forests that have remained untouched.

▲ *Tree kangaroos move about the branches very clumsily and have to descend tree trunks backward. This is a Grizzled tree kangaroo (Dendrolagus inustus).*

See also **Kangaroo**

KEY FACTS

● **Name**
Lumholtz's tree kangaroo (*Dendrolagus lumholtzi*)

● **Range**
Northeastern Queensland (Australia)

● **Habitat**
Mountainous rainforest near the coast

● **Appearance**
A small kangaroo, the head and body grow to 23 in (59 cm); a tail of 24-28 in (60-70 cm); a long, blackish-brown coat, paler on the belly, with the end half of the tail dark brown; the fore- and hind legs are similar in size; large feet with long, curved claws

● **Food**
Leaves and fruit

● **Breeding**
No definite breeding season; females give birth to a single young, although very little is known of the length of gestation or how long it spends inside its mother's pouch

● **Status**
Common within a limited range

Trout

KEY FACTS

● **Name**
Rainbow trout
(*Salmo gairdneri*)

● **Range**
Pacific coast of
North America, but
has been widely
introduced all over
the world

● **Habitat**
Fresh and coastal
waters where the
temperature is not
too high

● **Appearance**
Length up to 3$\frac{1}{4}$ ft
(1 m); the back may
be yellow-green,
blue-green or brown;
the sides and belly
are pale silver; a
broad rainbow
stripe along each
side, and black spots
on the back, sides,
and fins

● **Food**
Insect larvae, flying
insects, crustaceans,
snails; also other fish
and their eggs

● **Breeding**
Female lays up to
1000 eggs in each of
several nests; they
hatch in 4-7 weeks

● **Status**
Common

Members of the salmon family, trout and their close relatives the chars are native to the whole of the northern hemisphere. In addition, they have been introduced to suitable waters all over the world, and are also widely farmed for food.

Varying in size and color

Trout occur in a great variety of colors and sizes, depending on their habitat; as a result, they have been given many different names. The Shasta and Kamloops trout, for example, are just local varieties of the Rainbow trout found in the northwest; and the Steelhead is a form that migrates to and from the sea.

The Rainbow trout is native to the Pacific coast of the United States and Canada, where the streams and rivers run

▲ *Adult trout, like this Rainbow trout (Salmo gairdneri), feed on crustaceans, insects, snails, and other fish, their eggs, and their young.*

steeply down from the mountains to the sea. Although it varies greatly in color, it is recognizable by a broad rainbow stripe along each side and small black spots over the back, sides, and fins. Its back can be any color from yellow-green to brown, and its belly silver. The Steelhead, however, has a dark blue back and silvery sides and belly.

Most Rainbow trout spawn (breed) in the spring and the summer, from March through August. However, some spawn in the fall or even the winter. The male courts the female, who digs out a nest (known as a redd) in the gravel of the river bottom with sweeps of her tail. The two fish lie side by side and the female releases her large orange-yellow eggs into the redd, where the male fertilizes them with his sperm. Then the female covers them over with gravel.

Thousands of eggs

Females dig and spawn in several redds, releasing up to 1000 eggs in each. The eggs hatch in four to seven weeks (depending on how cold the water is) and for the first two weeks after hatching the young grow by absorbing the egg yolk. They then begin to swim and feed themselves, at which stage they are called parr. At first they feed on plankton (tiny water plants and animals), then gradually on larger crustaceans and snails on the river bottom. They also rise to the surface to feed on flying insects laying eggs.

Steelhead trout spawn in fresh water as Rainbow trout do, and the young spend their early lives there – usually two, but as much as four years. They then migrate to the sea, where they continue to grow in size, to as much as 4 ft (122 cm) in

length and 36 lb (16 kg) in weight. It may be several years before they return to fresh water to spawn.

The Brown trout (*Salmo trutta*) is native to Europe and western Asia, but like the Rainbow trout, it has been introduced around the world and is widely farmed. In habitat, breeding, and feeding it is very similar to the Rainbow trout, but it varies even more in size, from a few inches (cm) in length to over 37 in (95 cm).

Migrating to the sea

Like the Rainbow trout, the Brown trout has a migratory form, also known as the Sea trout. The young spend one to five years in fresh water before swimming down river to the sea, where they may live as many as five years before returning to the upper waters to spawn. The Sea trout grows large, and resembles the salmon, normally weighing at least 11 lb (5 kg). At sea it is a silver color with small black spots, but it darkens when it returns to fresh water.

▲ *These young fish are the offspring of the Brown trout* (Salmo trutta). *When they become adult, those Brown trout found in rivers and streams will not normally grow larger than 12-18 in (30-45 cm), weighing around 2¼ lb (1 kg). However, those found in lakes grow much larger and can reach weights as great as 22 lb (10 kg).*

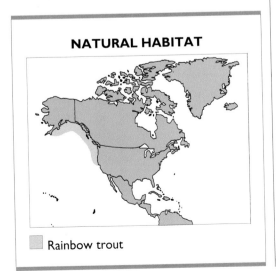

NATURAL HABITAT

Rainbow trout

Tuna

Tuna are members of the family *Scombridae*, which also includes the mackerels, and most species are fished commercially for food. They are found in the ocean worldwide, mainly in tropical and warm waters. However, they move into cooler waters during the summer and are regularly caught off the Nova Scotia coast, in the north Pacific, and in the seas south of Australia.

Most species are migratory, and travel in large schools over vast distances. Because it is possible to predict where the schools will appear at certain times of the year, fishing fleets are able to gather in those areas and there is serious overfishing. The flesh of most species is prized for food, but it is usually canned because it rots rapidly after death.

Fishing targets

There are several commercially important species. Perhaps the best known is the Bluefin tuna, which is found in the Atlantic ocean. The Skipjack tuna or Bonito (*Katsuwonus pelamis*), which is very

▲ *A streamlined body and large tail make the tuna a very powerful swimmer. In many species the fins can be folded down close to the body or into grooves to reduce water resistance. The Blue fin tuna can reach speeds of up to 50 mph (80 km/h).*

important to the California tuna fishing industry, is found in the Pacific Ocean. A third closely related species is the Yellowfin tuna (*Thunnus albacares*), which is fished extensively in the Indian Ocean.

Most tuna are blue or greenish on their backs and silvery on their sides and bellies, with very small scales. They have pointed snouts and large mouths with well-developed teeth. A series of small fins (finlets) runs between the fins on the back and between the fins below. Their tails are large and deeply forked.

Traveling through the ocean

Tuna are deep-sea fish, but come nearer the surface of the water in warmer weather, particularly on dark, still nights. The Bluefin and Yellowfin come closer to the shore at this time to spawn. The Bluefin lays eggs about 0.05 in (1.3 mm) in diameter; these have a globule of oil in them so that they float.

After hatching, the young travel in tight schools close to the surface. When they are not migrating adults tend to be solitary or form small schools. After spawning in the spring, the Bluefin gathers in larger schools and begins a long migration up the eastern coast of North America, appearing off the Bahamas in late April or early May, and by late summer they are as far north as Nova Scotia.

Tuna are also very popular as game fish, and the Bluefin features in several fishing competitions, such as the U.S. Atlantic Tuna Tournament and the Annual International Tuna Cup Match.

▼ *The Bluefin tuna (shown below) is the largest species of bony fish. At 3 years old it is already over 3¼ ft (1 m) long.*

KEY FACTS

● **Name**
Bluefin tuna or tunny (*Thunnus thynnus*)

● **Range**
Widely distributed in all oceans; found in cooler waters in the summer, moves to warm waters in the winter

● **Habitat**
Swims in schools near the surface of the water in the summer, coming close to the shore; lives in deeper water the rest of the year

● **Appearance**
Grows to 6½-10 ft (2-3 m), sometimes up to 13 ft (4 m), with a weight of 2000 lb (907 kg); at 3 years it is already over 3¼ ft (1 m) in length; dark blue to black above with silver sides and belly; a bright yellow band along each side

● **Food**
Schooling fish such as mackerel, anchovy, sardine, and herring; also squid

● **Breeding**
Spawns in inshore waters, April through August

● **Status**
Widespread

See also **Ocean**

Tundra

The tundra is a barren, icy, treeless region, most of which is situated within the Arctic Circle. Strong, chilling winds of up to 100 mph (160 km/h) sweep over the area almost constantly. This biome is so far north that the land is permanently frozen. As a consequence of its position on the earth, the tundra is shrouded in darkness in winter. During the summer, which lasts from six to eight weeks, the tundra is often overcast. Even on cloudless, summer days, sunlight is weak.

The average winter temperature in the tundra is about -13°F (-25°C). In summer the temperature rarely tops 50°F (10°C). Although blizzards and snowstorms are common for most of the year, the tundra is the second driest biome on the earth, after the desert. On average, the tundra gets 12 ins (30 cm) of rain per year, most of which falls in the summer.

Animals and vegetation that live in the tundra have to adapt to survive the harsh climate. Indeed, the tundra is one of the last truly wild places on earth.

Frozen soil

Since the temperature rarely exceeds freezing point (32°F/0°C), the subsoil is permanently frozen (permafrost). The permafrost layer lies just beneath the thin layer of surface soil and may be as much as 1 mile (1.6 km) deep.

Permafrost also prevents water from draining down into the earth. Instead, the tundra is streaked with streams and dotted with numerous bogs and ponds. Winter-

frozen soil partly thaws in summer. Such temperature variations cause the soil to contract and expand, breaking up the earth and creating surface cracks.

Hardy plants

Only low-lying vegetation that clings close to the ground can survive in the tundra, because in this position the vegetation is sheltered from the strong tundra winds. Most tundra plants have wide, shallow roots that collect liquid water from the thin layer of thawed soil above the permafrost.

Mosses are the main vegetation in the tundra because

▲ *Despite the harsh conditions of the Norwegian tundra, with its rocky surfaces and its thin layer of soil, the richly colored Alpine bearberry thrives during the six to eight week summer period.*

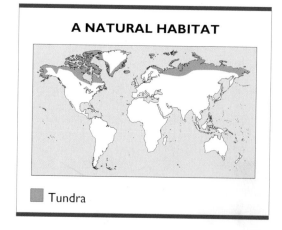

A NATURAL HABITAT

◼ Tundra

they can grow and reproduce quickly, when conditions are just right. Thick mats of mosses cover the tundra and insulate the ground. Many plants grow in these warm layers of moss.

There are approximately 2000 species of plants adapted to tundra life. Many are perennials, which means that they can live for many years. Flowering plants have to grow and reproduce quickly during the brief, sunlit summer, since this is the only time they can use energy from the sun to make the food they need to survive.

In summer, fields of beautifully colored wildflowers bloom in the tundra. Many flowers are big and showy to attract the rare insect pollinators. Their large, bowl-shaped blooms may also collect the sun's warmth.

Tundra trees have also adapted to the harsh conditions. They are unable to grow to their full size because their deep roots cannot penetrate the frozen soil. Instead, dwarf species of alder (*Alnus* spp.), birch (*Betula* spp.), and willow (*Salix* spp.) grow only a few inches off the ground.

Keeping warm

Most tundra animals are well insulated. The Musk ox (*Ovibos moschatus*) has an extremely thick and protective coat. The most common tundra plant-eater is the Greenland caribou (*Rangifer tarandus*). Both the Musk ox and the caribou avoid the worst of the winter by migrating south to the taiga. During the worst weather, some tundra plant-eaters, such as Arctic ground squirrels (*Citellus* spp.) and lemmings (*Lemmus* spp.), shelter in burrows beneath the ground.

By contrast, the Arctic hare (*Lepus timidus*) lives above ground all winter, foraging for food. Like birds such as the ptarmigan (*Lagopus mutus*) and the Willow grouse (*Lagopus lagopus*), the Arctic hare turns white in the winter to protect itself from predators such as the Arctic fox (*Alopex lagopus*), the ermine (*Mustela erminea*), the wolf (*Canis lupus*), and the wolverine (*Gulo gulo*). To help them stalk their prey unnoticed, Arctic foxes and ermines also turn white in winter.

Feeding and breeding

The tundra is a haven for migratory birds that come to breed and raise their young. Arctic terns (*Sterna paradisaea*), curlews (*Numenius* spp.), Semipalmated plovers (*Charadrius semipalmatus*), sandpipers (family *Scolopacidae*), and other waterfowl and shorebirds nest here. Many feast on the 3000 or so species of insects that swarm here in summer. Bloodsucking insects feast on birds, too, and on other animals.

However, bloodsuckers are a mere nuisance compared with the parasitic insects that lay eggs inside other animals' bodies. Some survive winter in their hosts' bodies; others are kept alive by a kind of antifreeze in their cells.

◄ *The plant-eating Musk ox (Ovibos moschatus) has a warm fur coat to insulate it from the tundra climate.*

See also **Moss, Musk ox, Polar regions, Taiga**

Turkey

Today, there are about 1.8 million wild turkeys in the U.S., living in woodlands and grasslands, and they can be found in almost every one of the states. It is thought that the Mexican Indians were the first to domesticate these birds. Domesticated turkeys were taken to Europe by the Spanish conquistadors in the early sixteenth century, and then brought back by early European settlers.

Increasing populations

At the end of the eighteenth century, there were approximately 10 million turkeys roaming the land, but by 1950 that number had been greatly reduced to only 300,000. Since then, thanks to the efforts of conservationists and laws that have restricted the activities of hunters, the turkey population has increased to its present level.

As well as being commonly found in the U.S., turkeys are also found in parts of Canada. Efforts have been made to

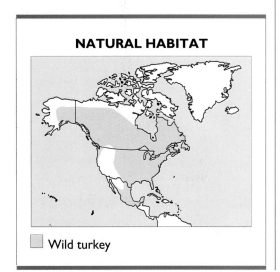

NATURAL HABITAT

☐ Wild turkey

establish the birds in Europe, but they have not always adjusted to the different environment as well as had been hoped. And although the turkey disappeared from much of its range in North America after the arrival of European settlers, who hunted it for food and destroyed its natural habitat, it has since been reintroduced into many of those places.

A large bird

Of all the birds found in North America, the turkey is one of the biggest. Wild turkeys can be 3-4 ft (1-1.2 m) tall, with males measuring up to 46 in (117 cm) in length and females 37 in (94 cm). There is a considerable difference in the weights of the sexes, with the males reaching an average weight of 22 lb (10 kg), and the females 9 lb (4 kg).

As you may expect from such a large bird, the turkey's legs are long and

▲ *Domestic turkeys that live on farms are mostly colored brown, red, or white. However, those that live in the wild are much darker and are usually black or brown with splashes of bright color. These two birds, photographed in Michigan, are male wild turkeys.*

powerful, and it tends to walk or run rather than fly. It is not quite flightless, but when it does fly, it is usually for short distances only.

At night flocks of turkeys roost in trees. They have a varied diet, consisting mainly of nuts, seeds, and berries, as well as a variety of small reptiles and invertebrates. Turkeys forage on the ground, mainly during early morning and late evening.

Males mate with several females. When it is time for them to attract a female, they perform spectacular courtship displays by fanning their tails and drooping and shaking their colorful flight feathers. Their head wattles also become swollen and brightly colored. They strut up and down, making loud gobbling noises. This behavior has sometimes led to them being nicknamed "gobblers."

A common scrape

After mating, the female goes off alone to build a nest, which is simply a scrape in the ground lined with leaves. The female usually lays about 10 eggs between February and July, although some females lay as few as eight and some as many as 20. It is also quite common for several females to lay their eggs in the same nest.

The female incubates the eggs for about one month, and the young are well developed when they hatch. They are then cared for by the female, who broods them at night for the first couple of weeks until they can fly. From then on they roost with the other birds in trees at night.

The young stay with their mother until they are about six months old. The young males then form a group and join up with other groups of brothers to form a flock. At this time they often fight each other, using their wings and spurs. Each individual fights to establish its position within its group and the group's position within the flock. Older birds are usually dominant over younger ones.

Females also form flocks, but they do not fight as much. The sexes live in these separate flocks over the winter, but at the beginning of the breeding season the large male flock again breaks up into groups. Males of the dominant groups have most matings and within each group only the top birds mate.

▲ *There are no feathers on the turkey's head but, with its red and blue markings, it is just as colorful as the rest of the bird's body. Hanging from the turkey's chin are some flaps of skin called wattles. All adult males, and some females, have "beards" made up of these wattles.*

Turtle

Turtles are water-loving reptiles that are very closely related to tortoises and terrapins and, with them, belong to a group known as the chelonians or testudines. Like their cousins, their bodies are protected by a bony shell that is covered with horn-like shields, and they have sprawling legs with short feet or flippers. They are toothless and usually eat soft foods, including plant material and animals such as worms, although some species have developed toughened jaws with which they can chew.

There are numerous species of turtle, all of which spend at least part of their time in water. As a general rule, those that live in fresh water are equally at home on land and in ponds, rivers, and lakes; but sea turtles spend almost all of their time in deep salty water, and come out onto land only to breed.

Freshwater turtles

The freshwater turtles vary enormously in appearance. They range from the tiny musk turtles, only about 4 in (10 cm) long, to the snapping turtles, which have shells up to 26 in (66 cm) long and can weigh up to 200 lb (90.7 kg). In most freshwater turtles the carapace (upper shell) is rather flattened, unlike those of the tortoises, which tend to be highly

NATURAL HABITAT

▢ Painted turtle
▣ Leatherback sea turtle

▲ *Painted turtles like these spend their time in the quiet waters of ponds, shallow lakes, and slow-moving streams. They are more aquatic (water dwelling) than many other species, although they like to bask in the morning and afternoon sun on a rock or log.*

▶ *Like other species of turtle, Painted turtles lay their eggs on land, in a nest dug in the earth. Once the young hatch, they make their way to water immediately.*

rounded. In some species the plastron (lower shell) covers only a small part of the body and these turtles cannot totally withdraw into their shells. The mud and musk turtles, however, have hinged lobes at the front and back of the shell that can be pulled shut when the turtle withdraws, so that it is completely enclosed by its protective casing.

Freshwater turtles are found on most continents except Antarctica. Those that are common in the United States include the Painted turtle and species of musk, mud, snapping, and soft-shelled turtles.

In quiet, shallow waters

Sometimes known as Pond turtles or Painted terrapins, there are four different subspecies of Painted turtle altogether, the most common of which is found in parts of southern Canada and much of the United States. Others are found in the valley of the Mississippi River, along parts of the east coast, and in the northeastern states. Typical of the freshwater turtles, the Painted turtle eats both plants and animals, although the bulk of its diet is made up of water plants. The animal portion of its food consists of insects and their larvae, snails, and fish.

Like Painted turtles, the mud and musk turtles prefer to live in the shallow, quiet waters of ponds and streams. They are rather similar to each other in appearance and habits. The mud turtles are often seen on land near very small pools or roadside ditches, but the Common musk turtle leaves its watery home very rarely. Both types of turtle have musk glands along the sides of their bodies, with the musk turtles giving off the strongest scent when they are alarmed or disturbed in some way. For this reason people have given the musk turtle the nickname "stinkpot."

Mud turtles only grow to about 6 in (15 cm), so they are not much larger than

KEY FACTS

- **Name**
  Painted turtle
  (*Chrysemys picta*)

- **Range**
  From the prairies of southern Canada and the northern U.S., south as far as New Mexico

- **Habitat**
  Ponds, the shallow edges of lakes, slow-moving streams

- **Appearance**
  Length 4-6 in (10-15 cm); an olive green carapace with yellow bands and red around the edge; the plastron is yellow with dark spirals and other marks; the head and neck have yellow lengthwise stripes; the legs are marked with red

- **Food**
  Aquatic plants, insects and their larvae, snails, tadpoles, fish

- **Breeding**
  The eggs are laid May-July in a nest dug in the earth; the newly hatched young are only 1 in (2.5 cm) long; they make their way to water almost immediately

- **Status**
  Widespread

musk turtles. Like musk turtles, they feed on insects, worms, tadpoles, and other small creatures, as well as stealing bait from fishermen.

Snapping jaws

Snapping turtles can inflict very painful bites if they are disturbed, and therefore should be treated with caution and respect. There are two species of snapping turtle, the Common snapping turtle and the Alligator turtle. The Alligator turtle, which occurs from Illinois to Texas and east to Florida, is among the largest of the world's freshwater turtles. It has a unique method of feeding. Instead of going in search of its prey, as the Common snapping turtle does, it lies still in the water, camouflaged by the algae (a mossy, plant-like growth) that grow on its shell. It lies with its mouth open, showing its tongue, which is divided at the front into two narrow forks. The turtle moves its tongue about so that the forks appear to

▼ Soft-shelled turtles, like this one, get their name because their shells are made of leathery skin rather than horn-like plates. These turtles spend much of their time under water, on the bottom of rivers and lakes. Then they push their long, tube-like snouts above the surface in order to take in air, or they rely on the gill-like structures in their mouths to absorb oxygen from the water. They have very strong jaws, covered by fleshy lips, and feed mainly on crayfish and water insects.

wiggle like worms. Unsuspecting fish swim into the turtle's mouth after the "prey" and the turtle then snaps its mouth shut.

Sea turtles

The sea turtles are marine reptiles that live in warm waters, although they are occasionally carried by currents into cooler regions. As a group they are larger than the freshwater turtles. Their limbs are well adapted for swimming and most sea turtles come ashore only to lay eggs. Although turtles and other chelonians have a reputation for being slow-moving, some of them can move at considerable speed in the water. For example, there are records of Green turtles swimming as far as 300 miles (480 km) in 10 days.

The Green turtle, which is found in the Indian Ocean and Caribbean Sea, may grow to 4½ ft (1.4 m) long and weigh up to 650 lb (290 kg). The largest sea turtle is the Leatherback turtle, which grows to 6 ft (1.8 m) in length and weighs a maximum of 1500 lb (680 kg). It breeds in Florida, the West Indies, and parts of South America and Asia.

One species of sea turtle is found farther north in the United States. The Hawksbill, which is distributed in all the tropical waters of the world, occurs as far north as Massachusetts in the Atlantic Ocean and Mexico in the Pacific. This sea turtle takes its name from its hooked "beak," which resembles that of the hawk. It feeds on crabs, fish, and aquatic plants, and also on jellyfish and Portuguese men-o'-war, which, although poisonous to many animals (including humans) do not seem to affect the turtle.

◀ *The process of egg laying for this female Leatherback sea turtle is long and difficult.*

KEY FACTS

• **Name**
Leatherback turtle
(*Dermochelys coriacea*)

• **Range**
Worldwide

• **Habitat**
Tropical seas;
occasionally
temperate and
subarctic seas

• **Appearance**
73 in (185 cm) long;
weighs 1500 lb
(680 kg); a long, dark
green carapace with
7 prominent ridges
running lengthwise;
broad, flipper-like
forelimbs

• **Food**
Crustaceans,
mollusks, jellyfish

• **Breeding**
During the breeding
season females lay
clutches of 50-170
eggs every 10 days
on sandy beaches;
the young turtles
measure 1½-2 in
(4-5 cm) when they
hatch; many do not
make it to the sea

• **Status**
Endangered

The Green turtle and the Hawksbill were once hunted and killed for their tasty flesh and used to make exotic dishes such as the popular turtle soup. The Hawksbill is also the source of tortoiseshell, much used in the past for decorative hair combs and other ornaments.

A long and difficult business
Like the Green turtle, the Hawksbill breeds in the Caribbean and the Indian Ocean, although these two species lay their eggs several months apart. Laying eggs is difficult and fairly lengthy for sea turtles, and the females use up a good deal of energy in the process.

The female turtle crawls up the beach and finds a suitable place beyond the high tide mark. She then digs a shallow hollow in the sand and, when this is complete, sets to work on the difficult part of the task. Using her hind flippers alternately to remove the sand, she digs an egg pit that is at least as deep as the length of her hind flippers, and in this she deposits about 100 eggs. When she has finished laying, she covers the pit over and firms the sand down. Finally she disguises the site by throwing sand loosely over it and returns to the sea, having spent several hours on the beach.

The length of the incubation period depends on the temperature, but generally the eggs hatch in about 50 days. The sex of the baby turtles also depends on the temperature at which they are incubated. Those eggs deep in the cool sand will produce females, and those in the warmer layers nearer the surface will produce males. As soon as the young turtles have dug their way out of the sand, they make their way down the beach to the sea. Many eggs never survive to the hatching stage because they are eaten by birds and mammals, as are many young sea turtles as they head for the sea.

See also **Lake, river, and estuary; Ocean**

Uakari

▲ *The Black-headed uakari (Cacajao melanocephalus) shown above has dark to reddish-brown fur covering its whole body, including its head. As a result, except for its short tail, it looks like many other South American monkeys.*

Uakaris are the only short-tailed primates in the New World. Scientists disagree about whether there are two or three species. Because the coat of the Bald uakari sometimes appears to be white and sometimes reddish-brown, the two forms are often classified as two separate species known as the White and Red uakaris.

The Bald uakari is found only in the swampy forest areas around the headwaters of the River Amazon and its connected rivers on the border between Brazil and Peru, where it lives in the treetops and rarely comes down to the ground. The Black-headed species is found further north, in northwestern Brazil and nearby in areas of Colombia and Venezuela. It lives in the forests of the Andean foothills, up to 1650 ft (500 m).

NATURAL HABITAT

Bald uakari

KEY FACTS

● **Name**
Bald, White,
or Red uakari
(*Cacajao calvus*)

● **Range**
Western Brazil to
parts of Peru

● **Habitat**
Lowland swamp
forests

● **Appearance**
Body 20-27 1/2 in
(51-70 cm); tail 4-6in
(10-15 cm); a long
shaggy coat and
beard, white to
reddish in color; the
face, forehead, and
crown is pink to
scarlet, with little
or no hair

● **Food**
Fruit, leaves, insects,
small mammals, birds

● **Breeding**
Live in mixed groups
of up to 30 males
and females; a single
young is born 6
months after mating

● **Status**
Endangered

▶ *With no hair on its forehead or crown, the Bald uakari looks like a worried, red-faced, old man. Its shaggy whitish coat and beard adds to the impression.*

Special adaptations

Because the atmosphere of the tropical forests is very moist and heavy to breathe, the uakaris' nostrils are adapted to prevent too much water filling their lungs. Their long hair also helps to protect them from the frequent heavy rain.

The uakaris are agile climbers, using their hands and feet, but they seldom leap from branch to branch like other monkeys because they do not have a long tail to give them balance when jumping.

They feed mostly on fruit, but also eat leaves, insects, small mammals such as bats and mice, and birds. To drink, they dip their hands into water and suck it from the long hairs. They often feed in groups with other species such as the Squirrel monkeys or the sakis.

Uakaris are active during the day, and gather in parties of up to 30, made up of several adult males, a harem of females, and their young. The females give birth to a single young after a pregnancy of about six months.

As well as the destruction of its forest habitat, humans are also contributing to the Bald uakari's declining numbers through hunting them for food and trapping them as pets for the export trade. Now scientists believe that all species of uakari are endangered.

Urban habitat

▲ *This Brown rat (Rattus norvegicus) is scavenging from a garbage can. Brown rats have an enormous appetite; they need to eat up to one third of their own body weight in food each day.*

As the human population grows ever larger, the earth's cities are expanding at an amazing rate. Densely populated areas of human habitation are called urban habitats. They have become home to wildlife as well as people. Urban areas actually comprise a number of different "habitats" – buildings, gardens, parks, sewers, and roads – which are attractive to a number of animals, plants, and other organisms. Some of these life-forms do very well here, even better than in their natural surroundings.

The effects of urbanization

As the development of buildings, roads, and other structures continues, more and more of the original habitat is destroyed. The original inhabitants are driven away unless they are able to adapt to the new surroundings. Urbanization allows other opportunistic species, which were not original inhabitants, to move in.

The most obvious effect of urbanization is the covering of fields with concrete. This can harm the animals that depended on those plants for food and shelter. For example, many birds need plants both for food and to build nests in which to lay their eggs. Any areas of vegetation that do remain are usually disturbed by the hustle and bustle of city life. Unless native plants can adapt to their changed surroundings, extinction is a very real possibility.

Another problem plants face is that much of the topsoil is removed during construction work. Consequently, urban soil is extremely low in nutrients. The soil is often so compacted that plants cannot push their roots through it, or it may be contaminated by chemical wastes, such as oils, gasoline, and pesticides.

Common urban animals

Many animals are a common sight in towns and cities. Birds, such as Purple martins (*Progne subis*), swallows (*Hirundo* spp.), and Peregrine falcons (*Falco peregrinus*) nest in the roofs of buildings. Ducks, pigeons, and swans are common in urban parks and, to some extent, are dependent on people who take time to feed them. Bees and wasps sometimes make their nests in lofts and wall cavities. Common and successful urban mammals include the Common raccoon (*Procyon lotor*), the Common opossum (*Didelphis virginiana*), and the Eastern gray squirrel (*Sciurus carolinensis*). In Europe, Red foxes (*Vulpes vulpes*) have successfully adapted to living in urban areas, scavenging on the remains from human garbage.

Adapting to survive

Despite the difficulties that animals face in urban habitats, many species do survive. Animals need to eat to survive. Biologists call plants producers, because they provide food for other organisms. However, many plant species cannot survive in urban areas, and those that do, such as algae, grasses, and mosses, are in very short supply. So how do the animals survive?

The most important factor that determines the success of an urban animal is adaptability. Urban life can be highly unpredictable. Those species that can adapt to change are far more successful than those that are sensitive to the 24-hour cycle of the city.

The ability to produce large numbers of offspring is also important to urban survival. City-dwelling animals face dangers such as automobiles and attacks by domestic dogs and cats. High levels of parasites and diseases in urban animals also tend to shorten their lifespan and reduce their numbers. A high reproduction rate

will replace individuals that die in such circumstances. In many cities the reproduction rate of some animals is so high that they are considered pests.

Human friend or foe?

The most successful city dwellers are usually those animals that have built up strong associations with humans. Buildings play a major role in this success. Just as apartments provide humans with shelter, they also create homes for rodents such as mice and rats (family *Muridae*) and insects such as the American cockroach (*Periplaneta americana*). Rodents and cockroaches live in hidden spaces. They avoid direct contact with people but come out at night to eat their food.

Humans consider these invaders as pests since are often found in sewers, where they can pick up diseases and then pass them on to people. Better sanitation and the development of antibiotics have greatly reduced the occurrence of disease. Efforts are also being made in many cities to return some urban land to a semi-natural state to attract more wildlife.

KEY FACTS

● **Plants**
Numerous plants cultivated in gardens, homes, parks, and along roadsides

● **Insects**
Ants, bees, butterflies, cockroaches, earwigs, fleas, flies, moths, wasps, and worms

● **Birds**
Crows, ducks, House sparrows, Peregrine falcons, pigeons, Purple martins, starlings, swallows, and swans

● **Mammals**
Badgers, hedgehogs, mice, opossums, raccoons, rats, Red foxes, and squirrels

▼ *At night the American cockroach creeps out of its hiding place in search of food.*

See also **Cockroach, Rat, Suburban habitat**

Venus flytrap

◄ *Each trap of the Venus flytrap has a very short life. Once it has caught and digested three or four insects, the trap dies.*

KEY FACTS

● **Name**
Venus flytrap
(*Dionaea muscipula*)

● **Range**
North and South Carolina

● **Habitat**
Bogs, ditches, and grasslands

Appearance
Low growing, with a ring of leaves at the base; flowering stem reaches to 18 in (45 cm); cluster of small, white flowers; 6-in- (15-cm-) long leaves with two lobes, hinged along the midline; three trigger hairs

● **Life cycle**
Perennial

● **Uses**
Ornamental and novelty interest

● **Status**
Endangered

The Venus flytrap (*Dionaea muscipula*), named after Venus, the Roman goddess of beauty, is perhaps the most famous meat-eating (carnivorous) plant in the world. Its dramatic hinged and sharp-spined leaves, reminiscent of steel traps, give it a fierce appearance. However, if you come across a Venus flytrap, there is no need to be afraid; this small, low-growing plant feeds mainly on crawling or flying insects. For this reason, it is more accurately described as an insect-eating (insectivorous) plant.

A tricky trap

The fearsome-looking traps of the Venus flytrap are the leaves. Each leaf blade has two round, kidney-shaped lobes, folded down the center and fringed with long,

spine-like hairs. When a leaf is open, or unfolded, the upper surface is visible, with its bright red color and three sensitive trigger hairs. The deadly trap is set and ready to spring.

Insects are attracted to the bright greens, reds, or yellows of the leaves and the scent of the nectar exuded around their edges. If an insect crawls or flies onto the surface and brushes against two trigger hairs at the same time, or one hair twice in the space of a few seconds, the two halves of the leaf snap shut in the blink of an eye. Taking just 1/30 of a second to close, even the most alert and rapid-moving flying insect cannot escape in time.

The mechanism is extremely specialized. The trap will not spring if the hairs are brushed by a nonliving object or force, such as a raindrop, a breeze, or a falling leaf. However, if a person accidentally touches the leaf, the trap will snap shut, reopening again within a few hours.

Despite its name, the Venus flytrap does not catch only flies, but also other insects such as ants, butterflies, and cockroaches. Very small insects can crawl out of the trap through the tiny spaces between the plant's interlocking spines, but once a larger creature is caught in the plant's embrace, its struggles simply serve to bring the two leaf blades closer together. This makes the trap even more secure. The movement of the unfortunate victim also stimulates the secretion of a digestive juice that kills and dissolves the insect. The leaf takes about ten days to absorb the rich food, after which it reopens, ready to take its next meal.

Endangered

Unfortunately, the Venus flytrap is no longer common in the wild. Its natural habitat is the sandy bogs of North and South Carolina. Many of these bogs are being drained to provide land in which to plant pine trees for timber. The Venus flytrap is now endangered. Many botanists believe it may even be extinct in the wild by the early twenty-first century. It is now a protected species in North Carolina.

Sundews

Although the Venus flytrap is the only one of its kind, it belongs to the much wider group of carnivorous plants known as the sundew family (*Droseraceae*), found all over the world in boggy and marshy habitats. One close cousin is the Waterwheel

plant (*Aldrovanda vesiculosa*), which, as its name suggests, is an aquatic meat-eating plant. It is found in Africa, Asia, Europe, and Australia. Sundews themselves (*Drosera* spp.) are tiny terrestrial, or land, plants, usually no bigger than 2 in (5 cm) across at their base. Their rounded, spatula-like leaves are covered with many upright hairs that secrete a glistening fluid to attract flying insects. This sticky liquid contains enzymes that begin to digest the trapped prey as soon as they become stuck to it.

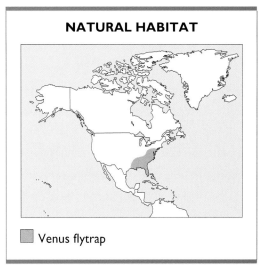

NATURAL HABITAT

☐ Venus flytrap

▼ *The leaves of the Venus flytrap (**Dionaea muscipula**) are fringed with sensitive, spine-like trigger hairs.*

See also **Bladderwort, Pitcher plant**

Viper

The Gaboon viper expects its meals to be served up at its door rather than having to go out looking for food. It lies heavily disguised on the floor of the rainforest, patiently waiting for some unlucky animal to pass its way. The viper then strikes to kill it quickly, using a means of attack that will give its prey little chance of fighting or seeking escape.

Huge fangs

When the prey is in sight, the Gaboon viper swiftly lifts its head, opens its mouth wide and erects its deadly fangs before sinking them into its victim's body. Its fangs are the longest of any snake and can be more than 2 in (5 cm) in length. Vipers use their fangs to stab rather than bite their prey, injecting venom into its body. The Gaboon viper takes a variety of prey, such as ground birds and mammals, including small antelopes and porcupines.

All vipers are venomous. They have a pair of long, hollow teeth, or fangs, through which poison travels whenever they make a strike. When these are not in use the viper keeps them folded flat against the roof of its mouth. At the point of attack, the viper has the ability to erect both of its fangs at the same time or to erect just one if that is all that is needed. Each fang has a series of replacements behind it and, as each new fang develops, the old one loosens and either falls out or is left embedded in the viper's victim.

The Gaboon viper is one of the largest of all snakes. An average-sized adult is 3-4 ft (0.9-1.2 m) long. Females grow

KEY FACTS

- **Name**
  Gaboon viper
  (*Bitis gabonica*)

- **Range**
  Central Africa

- **Habitat**
  Rainforests

- **Appearance**
  Adults are 3-4 ft
  (0.9-1.2 m) long on
  average; their skin is
  patterned with
  brown, yellow, black,
  and purple

- **Food**
  Ground birds and
  mammals

- **Breeding**
  Average of 24 young
  are born live

- **Status**
  Widespread

◄ *One of the world's most dangerous snakes, the Puff adder gets its name from its habit of rearing up and puffing itself up like a long balloon when threatened. This viper is found in parts of Africa and the Middle East.*

larger than males, and some females can grow up to 7 ft (2 m) in length. The Gaboon viper's head is broad, and its nose contains horns, although the purpose of these horns is not known.

Cryptic coloring

In its natural habitat of the rainforest floor, it is very important that the Gaboon viper is able to blend in successfully with the fallen leaves and other debris that make up its surroundings. Its coloring is the main thing that helps it to do this. The patterns on its skin of brown, yellow, black, and purple perfectly camouflage it in the dappled light of the forest floor.

Because the Gaboon viper is such a big snake it requires a lot of effort and energy to move around the rainforest. However, when it needs to the viper is able to very quickly move away from danger, or even pursue a victim.

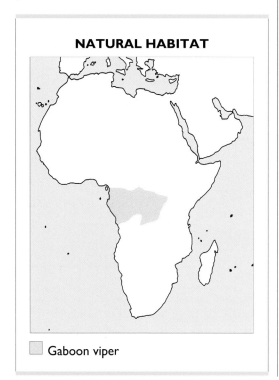

NATURAL HABITAT

Gaboon viper

Many young

There are about 180 different species of viper throughout the world. Most species give birth to live young, although some species do lay eggs. The Gaboon viper gives birth to as many as 60 young, although on average the number is usually fewer than 24. The young are 10-12 in (25-30.5 cm) long, with similar colors and markings to the adults.

There are three subfamilies of vipers: the *Viperinae*; the *Crotalinae*; and the *Azemiopinae*. The *Viperinae* are the "true vipers" of the Old World. This family includes the Gaboon viper, the Saw-scaled viper (*Echis carinatus*), and the Puff adder (*Bitis arietans*).

The *Crotalinae* include the rattlesnakes and pit vipers of Asia and America. Pit vipers have a deep facial pit on each side of the head, between the eye and the nostril. This is an organ that they use to sense warm-blooded prey. The *Azemiopinae* is the most basic subfamily, and only contains one species, the very rare Fea's Viper (*Azemiops feae*) from Asia.

▲ *The patterning and coloring of this Gaboon viper in South Africa means that it is very difficult to see on the forest floor. This means that humans often step upon them accidentally. The venom from a Gaboon viper can be fatal to people.*

See also **Rattlesnake**

Index

A

Adder, Puff 958, 959
Alligator turtle 950
American bullfrog 930
American cockroach 955
American mink 903
American toad 930, 931
Aracari 936, 937
Arctic hare 945
Arctic tern 922, 923, 945
Assam tea 712, 713

B

Badger 917
Baird's tapir 906
Bald (Red or White) uakari
  952, 953
Barnacle 926–927
Bear
  Black 903
  Grizzly 903
Bearberry 944
Bird-eating spider 909
Black bear 903
Black-headed uakari 952
Bluefin tuna (tunny) 942, 943
Boar, Wild 917
Brazilian (South American)
  tapir 906, 907
Brown creeper 917
Bull frog 930
Burrowing toad 931

CDE

Capercaillie 903
Coast 926–927
Cockroach 955
Common midwife toad 931
Common musk turtle 949
Common snapping turtle 950
Common (Tailless) tenrec
  918–919
Cotton-top tamarin 905
Dahurian larch 902–903
Desert tarantula 908, 909
Diamond-back terrapin
  924–925

Dingo 911
Domestic turkey 946
Dormouse 917
Eggplant 932

FG

Fea's viper 959
Forest, temperate 914–917
Freshwater turtle 948–949
Frog 930
Gaboon viper 958–959
Geographic terrapin 924
Giant marine toad 931
Giant tortoise 935
Golden-headed tamarin 904
Goliath bird-eating spider 909
Gooseneck barnacle 927
Gopher tortoise 934–935
Gray wolf 903, 945
Greater hedgehog tenrec 918
Great gray owl 915
Great plains toad 931
Green turtle 950, 951
Grizzly bear 903

H–L

Hare, Arctic 945
Harvester termite 921
Hawksbill turtle 950, 951
Houston toad 931
Irish moss 926
Jay, Stellar's 916–917
Larch 902–903
Leatherback turtle 948, 950
Lesser hedgehog tenrec 918,
Lichen 902, 926
Lion tamarin 904
Lumholtz's tree kangaroo
  938
Lynx 903

M

Malayan tapir 906
Map terrapin 924

Marmoset 904
Midwife toad 931
Mink, American 903
Moss 944–945
Mountain tapir 906
Mountain toucan 937
Mud turtle 949–950
Musk ox 945
Musk turtle 948, 949

N–R

Northern flying squirrel 903
Nuthatch 917
Ox, Musk 945
Owl 915
Painted terrapin 949
Painted turtle 948, 949
Pit viper 959
Pond turtle 949
Puff adder 958, 959
Rainbow trout 940–941
Rattlesnake 959
Red (Bald or White) uakari
  952, 953

S

Sable 903
Sea trout 941
Skipjack tuna 942–943
Snapping turtle 948, 949,
  950
Soft-shelled turtle 950
Sooty tern 922
South American (Brazilian)
  tapir 906, 907
Spadefoot toad 931
Spider, bird-eating 909
Squirrel, Northern flying
  903
Steelhead trout 940, 941
Stellar's jay 916–917
Sumatran tiger 928
Sundew 957
Surinam toad 931

T

Taiga 902–903
Tailless (Common) tenrec
  918–919
Tamarin 904–905
Tapir 906–907
Tarantula 908–909
Tasmanian devil 910–911
Tea 912–913
Temperate forest 914–917
Tenrec 918–919
Termite 920–921
Tern 922–923
Terrapin 924–925
Tide pool and coast 926–927
Tiger 907, 928–929
Toad 930–931
Toco toucan 936, 937
Tomato 932–933
Tortoise 934–935
Toucan 936–937
Toucanet 936, 937
Tree kangaroo 938–939
Trout 940–941
Tuna 942–943
Tundra 944–945
Tunny (Bluefin tuna) 942,
  943
Turkey 946–947
Turtle 948–951

U–Z

Uakari 952–953
Urban habitat 954–955
Venus flytrap 956–957
Viper 958–959
Waterwheel plant 957
West African live-bearing
  toad 931
White tern 923
White (Bald or Red) uakari
  952, 953
Wild boar 917
Wild turkey 946–947
Wolf 903, 917, 945
Woodpecker 917
Yellowfin tuna 943

Page numbers in **boldface type** show full articles